THE PISCATAQUA VALLEY
IN THE AGE OF SAIL

THE PISCATAQUA VALLEY

IN THE AGE OF SAIL

A BRIEF HISTORY

Russell M. Lawson, PhD

Charleston   London

History
PRESS

Published by The History Press
Charleston, SC 29403
www.historypress.net

Front cover: Fort Constitution is now a historic site situated on the grounds of the U.S. Coast Guard. *Courtesy of Benjamin Lawson.*
Back cover: Once known as the Old South Meetinghouse, housing the first parish of Portsmouth, this building is today used for the Portsmouth Children's Museum. *Courtesy of Benjamin Lawson.*
Fontispiece: Whaleback Light at the mouth of the Piscataqua. This view is from the early 1900s. *From* Vignettes of Portsmouth.

First published 2007

Manufactured in the United Kingdom

ISBN 978.1.59629.219.2

Library of Congress Cataloging-in-Publication Data

Lawson, Russell M., 1957-
  The Piscataqua Valley in the age of sail, 1600-1900 / Russell M. Lawson.
    p. cm.
  Includes bibliographical references.
  ISBN 978-1-59629-219-2 (alk. paper)
1. Piscataqua River Valley (N.H. and Me.)--History. 2. Piscataqua River Valley (N.H. and Me.)--History, Military. 3. Piscataqua River Valley (N.H. and Me.)--Commerce--History. 4. Shipbuilding--Piscataqua River Valley (N.H. and Me.)--History. 5. Piscataqua River Valley (N.H. and Me.)--Intellectual life. I. Title.
  F42.P4L39 2007
  974.2'6--dc22
                                    2007009410

FOR LINDA

CONTENTS

INTRODUCTION

The Piscataqua Valley from 1600 to 1900 was the focus of trade, shipbuilding and fishing of northern New England. Marine activities were centered at Portsmouth on the southern shores of the Piscataqua and at Kittery, across the river opposite Portsmouth. Upstream on the upper Piscataqua and its tributaries were diverse shipbuilding, fishing and lumber towns, especially Newington on the Piscataqua, Salmon Falls and Berwick on the Salmon Falls River, Dover on the Cocheco River, Newmarket on the Lamprey River, Durham on the Oyster River and Exeter and Stratham on the Squamscot River. The Lamprey and Squamscot Rivers form the Great Bay, a beautiful estuary that in the colonial period provided secure coves for shipyards and sawmills.

The Piscataqua Valley basin drains close to a thousand square miles. It ranges from as far west as the Squamscot Valley, which extends to Chester, Brentwood and Fremont. The watershed from which the Squamscot springs includes ridges between Exeter and Hampton, between Sandown and Hampstead and between Brentwood and Kingston. The Lamprey River extends west to Epping, Candia, Deerfield and Northwood; it springs from the watershed between East Candia and Candia and between Northwood and Epsom. The Oyster River reaches west to Lee and Madbury. The Cocheco River extends northwest to Strafford, Rochester, Farmington and New Durham, rising along the Blue Hill Range north of Strafford, and the ridge between New Durham and Middleton. The Salmon Falls River extends north to Wakefield and Sanbornville, and northeast to Sanford and the Berwicks, rising along the ridge around Wakefield and Sanbornville and the ridge separating Sanborn from Springvale. The Piscataqua also drains the watersheds between South Sanford and Kennebunk, and the ridge separating York from Kittery.

Native American tribes such as the Piscataqua, Squamscot and Newichawannock inhabited the Piscataqua Valley when in 1603 the first English ship sailed up the Piscataqua River, captained by Martin Pring. Other early adventurers to the region were John Thomson, who settled at Odiorne Point; Edward Hilton, who settled at Dover Point; and Walter Neal, the representative of the first proprietors, John Mason and

Ferdinand Gorges, who called the land Laconia. The towns of the upper Piscataqua Valley were settled during the 1600s by land speculators, fishermen and merchants from England and Puritans from Massachusetts.

Piscataqua towns played an important role in the wars for empire of the 1600s and 1700s, such as King William's War (1689–97), Queen Anne's War (1703–13), Dummer's War (1722–25), King George's War (1744–49) and the French and Indian War (1755–63). Piscataqua towns built fortifications to defend themselves with mixed success against French and Indian attacks. Towns near the hinterland, such as Durham, Exeter and Dover, were frequently attacked by French soldiers and their Indian allies, and just as often retaliated with local militia, led by the likes of Major Robert Rogers, marching up rivers and streams into the inland forest. The most exciting military adventure occurred in 1745, when William Pepperrell led New England militia on the conquest of the French fort of Louisburg at Cape Breton.

Fort Constitution is now a historic site situated on the grounds of the U.S. Coast Guard. *Courtesy of Benjamin Lawson.*

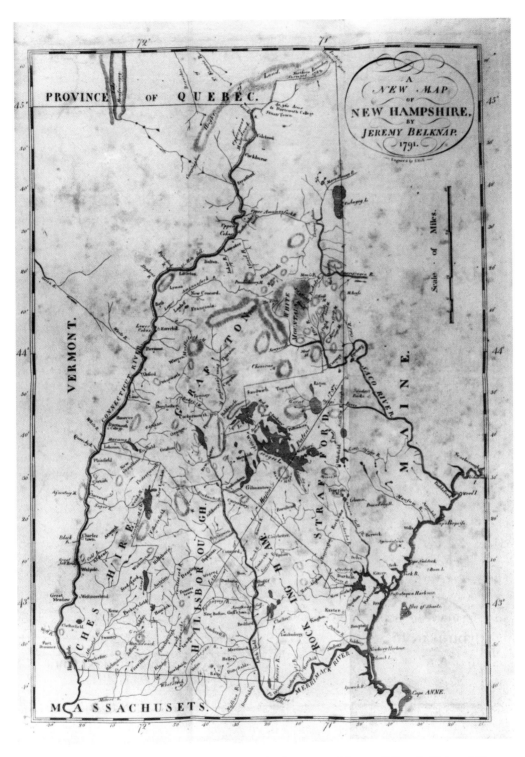

This detailed map of New Hampshire accompanied volume two of Jeremy Belknap's *History of New Hampshire*, published in 1791. *Courtesy of Dartmouth College Library.*

The first aggressive action of the American Revolution occurred at Newcastle at the mouth of the Piscataqua, when in 1774 American soldiers led by Portsmouth resident John Langdon and Durham resident John Sullivan captured Fort William and Mary from the British. Portsmouth, Kittery and towns upstream (such as Exeter) were centers of shipbuilding and privateering during the war. John Paul Jones stayed at Portsmouth on several occasions waiting for the outfitting of his ships *Ranger* and *America*. Scientist and historian Jeremy Belknap wrote of the war and its causes from his home in Dover. Portsmouth and Exeter served as colonial, Revolutionary and early national capitals of the colony and state of New Hampshire. Portsmouth merchants John Langdon and William Whipple were signers of the Declaration of Independence.

During the early 1800s, the Piscataqua became a center of a reinvigorated American shipbuilding industry. The Portsmouth Naval Shipyard, still in operation, was founded in 1800 on an island on the Maine side of the river. Piscataqua shipyards built clipper ships by the 1830s and ironclads by the 1860s. Towns such as Newmarket and Dover became manufacturing centers, while Durham became an intellectual center as the home of the University of New Hampshire. The beauty of the Piscataqua Valley became the subject of art, poetry and prose, inspiring artists such as Childe Hassam, writers such as Nathaniel Hawthorne, Thomas Bailey Aldrich and Sarah Orne Jewett, and poets such as Celia Laighton Thaxter.

There are a host of useful literary sources to recreate the history of the Piscataqua Valley from 1600 to 1900. These include the accounts of explorers such as Martin Pring, who wrote a narrative of his journey up the Piscataqua. John Smith explored coastal Maine and New Hampshire and wrote several books about his experiences, notably *The Description of New England*. English scientist and physician John Josselyn journeyed twice to the Piscataqua Valley during the 1630s and 1660s, which led to two publications, *New-Englands Rarities Discovered* and *Two Voyages to New-England*. The Piscataqua Valley has had numerous contemporary historical accounts as well, such as James Sullivan's *History of the District of Maine*, Nathaniel Adams's *Annals of Portsmouth*, Charles Brewster's *Rambles About Portsmouth*, Sarah Orne Jewett's *The Old Town of Berwick* and Thomas Bailey Aldrich's *An Old Town by the Sea*.

Foremost among contemporary writings is the three-volume *History of New-Hampshire*, published in 1784, 1791 and 1792 by the clergyman and scientist Jeremy Belknap, who lived at Dover and explored the Piscataqua Valley from 1767 to 1786. Belknap was a natural as well as a human historian; the first two volumes of his *History of New-Hampshire* provides an extensive narrative of the history of the Piscataqua from the first English explorers of the early 1600s to the War for Independence and creation of the independent state of New Hampshire during the 1770s and 1780s. Volume three of Belknap's *History* is a encyclopedic discussion of the geography, landscape, flora, fauna, settlements, economy and culture of New Hampshire in general and the Piscataqua Basin in particular.

Chapter One

The Piscataqua

The Piscataqua is a short but powerful river. At its mouth sea and river merge, brine with fresh water, amid churning waves spawned by the competition of incoming tide and the inexorable flow of water from inland to sea. Where river ends and sea begins is indistinct. The mariner sailing along the coast north to south perceives a broad indentation in the land, the entrance to a bay or river. The suspicion that it is the latter grows with the smell and taste of fresh water and the competing currents. If the day is clear the mariner sees that the coast recedes and sea gives way to islands and promontories. But if fog layers the surface of the water, the hints of a great river inland are forgotten in the quest to avoid shoals and shipwreck.

Spying the mouth of the Piscataqua from the sea can be difficult, as illustrated by the experiences of Captain John Smith, who sailed the waters of coastal Maine and New Hampshire in 1614. A perceptive explorer, Smith had that summer found and sailed up the Penobscot and Kennebec rivers of Maine. He explored Cape Elizabeth and Cape Ann and made port at the Isles of Shoals, which lie a few miles to the east of the mouth of the Piscataqua. But in his many writings about coastal New England, such as *A Description of New England* (1616), Smith did not mention exploring the Piscataqua. Seeking harbors, bays and rivers to host a colony, Smith's silence was not purposeful. The day was hazy perhaps, or the attention of the mariners was drawn more to the eight islands off the coast that make up the Isles of Shoals. For whatever reason, Smith failed to explore one of the best harbors on the East Coast.

Others were more fortunate. European explorers began coasting along the waters of Maine and New Hampshire as early as the 1520s, when the Italian Giovanni Verrazano sailed up the coast from South Carolina to Maine. Others followed in his wake, particularly fishermen from west country towns of England such as Bristol, or the port cities along the French coast such as Rouen and Dieppe, or Basque fishermen making their way across the Atlantic from the Bay of Biscay. The Portuguese explorer Esteban Gómez in 1525, the English explorers John Rut in 1527 and Bartholomew Gosnold in 1602, and the French explorer Samuel de Champlain in 1604 explored these waters.

But it was the voyage of Martin Pring in 1603 that provided the first glimpse, if brief and shadowy, of the Piscataqua Valley.

THE VOYAGE OF MARTIN PRING

Martin Pring was a young man of twenty-three when Bristol (England) merchants gave him command over two ships, the *Speedwell* and the *Discover*. The former was a bark of fifty tons burden, the latter a pinnace of twenty-six tons. In April 1603, they set sail from England, arriving off the coast of Maine in June. Pring explored three rivers on the Maine coast before arriving at the Piscataqua. In Pring's account of the voyage, written years later, he recalled that of the rivers they spied, "the fourth and most Westerly was the best, which we rowed up ten or twelve miles." Pring and his men discovered that the Piscataqua was one of the most difficult rivers they had ever sailed. The river—draining a region of hundreds of acres and fed by seven significant rivers and innumerable springs, with a strong east wind and high tides competing with the descending flow of fresh water—is one of the most rapid large rivers in the world. The currents are strong and tricky, the hazards many, the fog frequent and the navigable channels mystifying. Pring's account of his voyage up the Piscataqua is brief and vague. The entrance to the Piscataqua is between two great apparent headlands, though both are large islands separated from the mainland by small channels. Between Newcastle Island to the west and Gerrish Island to the east, the river channel is less than a mile wide and thirty feet deep with up to ten-foot tides and six-knot winds. Somehow, both bark and pinnace made their way gingerly but safely. Along the way Pring saw several excellent harbors, at one of which he presumably ordered that the larger bark, *Speedwell*, ride at anchor. Meanwhile Pring and a small number of adventurers rowed the small pinnace *Discover* upstream. A pinnace was a smaller version of a bark; though both were relatively small boats, they possessed three masts, the square foremast at bow, the lateen mizzenmast at stern and the square mainmast emerging from the center waist of the boat. The pinnace had a shallow draft and hence was good at river navigation, though Pring was a sufficiently knowledgeable mariner who realized that to try to ascend the Piscataqua under sail with the wind to stern would be courting disaster. So the men furled the sails and took to the oars.

The broad mouth of the river narrows into a maze of islands, jagged shoreline, bays and inlets. Pring and his men rowed against the current, seeking the main channel, passing by likely harbors, good defensible promontories and rich, forested land. Pring's narrative gives no indication of how long it took the English to ascend the river, how long they stayed and where precisely they went. The narrative does make clear that they anchored and went ashore to explore the land. The object of Pring's voyage was commercial—to discover, harvest and return to England as much sassafras as he could find and his two boats could hold. Sassafras is a tree that grows in poor, moist soil. Although it can reach one hundred feet in height, the sassafras of New Hampshire is a small tree. "Its root, bark and leaves have an aromatic smell," wrote Jeremy Belknap. "It affords a valuable ingredient for beer as well as for medicinal purposes." Native Americans made tea from its bark and roots to treat a variety of ailments of the intestines as well as arthritis. The English had come to prize the tree for its curative properties. Bartholomew Gosnold in the previous year of 1602 had sailed the New England coast looking in part for sassafras, which he found in great abundance in southern New England. A member of Pring's crew, who had sailed with Gosnold, was among the shore party that, during the frequent stops to explore the inland forests and swamps, sought in vain for sassafras. Nevertheless they discovered "very goodly Groves and Woods replenished with tall Okes, Beeches, Pine-trees, Firre-trees, Hasels, Wich-hasels and Maples." The forests of the Piscataqua Valley hosted plentiful wildlife as well. The English saw, even on so brief a visit, "sundry sorts of Beasts, as Stags, Deere, Beares, Wolves, Foxes, Lusernes, and Dogges with sharpe noses." Pring hoped to find people as well, to find out what was their way of life and whether there was evidence that they possessed sassafras. However, "in all these places we found no people, but signes of fire where they had beene."

Indeed, the Piscataqua Valley hosted several Indian tribes: the Piscataqua tribe lived on the upper Piscataqua River near Dover Point, the Squamscot tribe on the Squamscot River near Exeter and the Newichawannock tribe on the Newichawannock or Salmon Falls River near Berwick. If Pring was accurate in his claim that the English rowed "ten or twelve miles" up the Piscataqua, then they ascended the Piscataqua to Dover Point, where it meets the waters of Little Bay and Great Bay formed by the Bellamy (Back), Oyster, Lamprey and Squamscot Rivers. Dover Point is, in Belknap's words, "an high neck of land between the main branch of Pascataqua and Back river, about two miles long, and a half a mile wide, rising gently along a fine road, and declining on each side like a ship's deck. It commands an extensive and variegated prospect of the rivers, bays, adjacent shores, and distant mountains." If Pring and his men explored Dover Point, which the Indians called Winnichahannat, they found no signs of the Piscataquas, whose absence from the English could have been by design; or, the tribe could have gone upstream to Cocheco Falls to fish. If the English turned west at Dover Point, they sailed through a treacherous channel between Bloody and Dover Points into a rapid current formed by the mouths of the Bellamy and Oyster Rivers, both of which are small rivers that rise about fifteen miles inland. Passing these the English entered Little Bay, then Great Bay, five miles long and three miles wide, formed in part by the waters of the Lamprey and Squamscot Rivers. At high tide, according to one nineteenth-century observer, "when this large basin is filled by the sea, the prospect over its pellucid surface, framed all around with green meadows and waving grain and noble woods, is truly enchanting. But when the tide is out, a vast bed of black ooze is exposed to view, bearing the scanty waters of several small streams which empty into this great lagune," such streams including Pickering Brook and the Winnicut River, flowing from Greenland. The mouth of the Squamscot is twenty-five miles from the sea. Up the Squamscot River about six miles are the falls where the Squamscot tribe, led by the sachem Wehanownowit, fished for salmon. Beyond these falls, the Exeter River extends into the forested interior about forty miles. The Lamprey River, like the Squamscot, is tidal, rising and falling with the tide below the lower falls. Upstream, the river extends over forty miles, broken by numerous falls where the fishing is good, such as at Packer's Falls. The Lamprey is fed by the Little River and the Piscassic River.

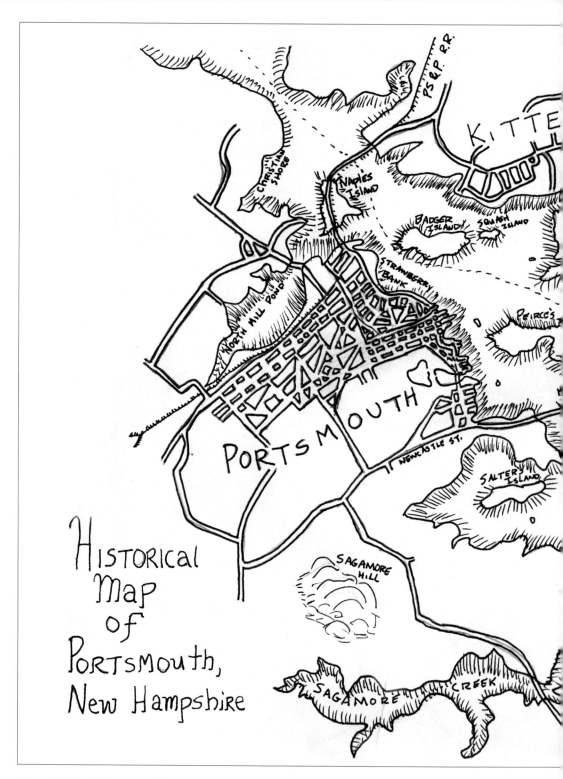

Historical Map of Portsmouth. The mouth of the Piscataqua, as shown in this map by Benjamin Lawson, was a maze of islands that to navigate challenged the most able mariner. *Courtesy of Benjamin Lawson.*

Pring and his men at Dover Point more likely turned north following the main channel of the Piscataqua, which proceeds several miles to the mouths of the Cocheco and Newichawannock rivers. Had the English ascended either of these rivers, they would have, perchance, discovered the Newichawannock tribe at Salmon Falls or the Piscataqua tribe at Cocheco Falls fishing for salmon.

Every spring, the early seventeenth-century sachem of the Newichawannock tribe, Rowls, repaired to the point, which they called Quampeagan, that separated the Newichawannock from a tributary, the Asbenbedick (Great Falls) River. At these falls of about thirty feet, salmon was so plentiful that, according to one legend preserved by Sarah Orne Jewett, "one might walk across on the salmon, which wedged themselves into solid masses in their efforts to leap the impossible high fall near the mouth of Chadbourne's or the Great Works River." Above the falls, the Newichawannock extends over thirty miles and the Asbenbedick twenty-seven miles. From Quampeagan to the mouth of the Cocheco is four miles.

The falls of the Cocheco ("rapid falling water"), a drop of thirty-four feet, are just a few miles upstream from the confluence with the Piscataqua River, easily reached by Pring and his men by land trails or, preferably, birch bark canoe. Above the falls the Cocheco extends inland over thirty miles, fed by beautiful forest streams such as the Isinglass River, the Ela River and the Mad River. The Piscataqua tribe arrived at the falls in late spring and early summer, which was the best time to fish for salmon in river waters, when the fish struggled upstream to spawn. The whole tribe relocated for a time to the falls, the men engaged in fishing, the women in cleaning and drying or smoking the fish. In shallow water just below the falls, men positioned boulders or drove wooden stakes at intervals across the width of the stream, then stretched nets or placed woven brushwood from stake to stake, forming a weir. At one place they left an opening for the fish to ascend the river; the salmon, arriving at the rushing current at the falls, retreated downstream until trapped by the weir. Then it was a simple task for the men to spear the salmon. Huge quantities of fish were taken and deposited on shore for the women. Feasting and merriment followed in the evening hours.

At other times of the year Indians fished at night using pitch torches, spears and nets. Belknap wrote that Piscataqua Valley fishermen of his time continued to use the Indian techniques:

> *A lighted pitch-knot is placed on the outside of a canoe, which not only attracts the fish, but gives the fishermen direction where to strike. The river is sometimes illuminated by a multitude of these floating lights. The Indian scoop-net is shaped like a pocket; the edge of which is fastened to a wooden bow, at the end of a long pole. With these are caught salmon, shad, alewives, smelts, and lampreys. Frost-fish are taken with wooden tongs, and black eels in cylindrical baskets, with a hole, resembling mouse traps made of wire.*

Bass were speared in forest ponds, which yielded the Indian delicacy upaquontop, a stew made of bass head and hominy. The tidal basin of the Piscataqua Valley yielded numerous shellfish upon which Indians feasted.

Upriver from Dover Point, the Piscataqua is fed by the Cocheco River, upon which were built the towns of Dover and Rochester. *Photo by author.*

Piscataqua River, approaching Portsmouth. The Piscataqua is a river of rapid currents and high tides and is notable for never freezing, notwithstanding the harshest winter. *Photo by author.*

Besides fish, there was plentiful wildlife in the inland forests of the Piscataqua Valley. Native hunters were expert at the use of bow and arrow, spear, axe and knife. They did not have horses, but hunted on foot. Sometimes the hunter pursued prey alone, but just as often the whole tribe of men participated in the hunt. One technique was to drive animals into a narrow triangular space, such as a point jutting into a river, where, trapped in a confined space, the animals were easy to bring down with bow and arrow. The Squamscot tribe did this at Fox Point, which juts into Little Bay. Belknap wrote that in August, when "old ducks shed their feathers, and the young, being unfledged, are not able to fly," they are "driven into small creeks, whence they cannot escape. They are then easily caught in great numbers, and preserved for winter by salt or smoke." The Indians also devised intricate traps to take game. An example is the culheag, which, according to Belknap, who had examined one,

> is a forceps, composed of two long sticks, one lying on the other, connected at one end, and open at the other…In this enclosure is placed the bait, fastened to a round stick, which lies across the lower log, the upper log resting on the end of a perpendicular pointed stick…The animal having scented the bait, finds no way to come at it, but by putting his head between the logs. As soon as he touches the bait, the round stick, on which it is fastened, rolls; the perpendicular gives way; the upper log falls, and crushes him to death in an instant, without injuring his skin.

The culheag allowed the Indian hunter to clothe himself and his family in the warm, durable furs of the ermine, raccoon, beaver, wolverine, rabbit, lynx, mink and martin. Bow and arrow and spears yielded deer meat and skin for use in clothing and moccasins, bear meat and grease and moose hide, which was useful in making canoes when the bark of the white birch was not available.

Martin Pring's list of trees observed at the Piscataqua—"Okes, Beeches, Pine-trees, Firre-trees, Hasels, Wich-hasels and Maples"—strangely did not include the paper birch, perhaps because the tree is native to North America, hence was unfamiliar to the English. The paper birch was one of the most useful trees in Indian material culture. Indians (and colonists, after learning the technique) stripped the long sheets of tough, pliable bark from the tree, formed it around a frame made of cedar, sewed the bark with fibrous black spruce roots and sealed it with pine resin. Such canoes were light but could hold the weight of many warriors and their weapons, were convenient to port around falls and were easily repaired from the materials of the forest. Indian craftsmen used birch bark to fashion cookery and baskets, and to make snug wigwams that kept out the cold and precipitation. The medicinal qualities of the birch included treatment of fever, infections and arthritis.

By the time the English came to the Piscataqua Valley, Indian healers had developed a pharmacoepia based on the materials of the forest. Of the different varieties of oak trees found in New Hampshire, the Indians prized the white oak for its antiviral and antiseptic medicinal qualities; natives made tea from the bark for medicine or gargle.

A nineteenth-century print of Passaconaway, chief of the Penacook tribe of the Merrimack Valley, whose influence during the first half of the seventeenth century extended even to the Piscataqua Valley. *From Charles Beals's* Passaconaway in the White Mountains. *Courtesy of Benjamin Lawson.*

Indians treated asthma, burns and rashes with tea and poultices made from the bark and leaves of the American beech, which Pring saw growing along the Piscataqua. Poultices and tea made from the bark, leaves and pitch of the massive white pine, which towered about Piscataqua Valley rivers and streams, helped Indians with numerous physical complaints: wounds, boils, colds and arthritis. "Firre-trees," namely the balsam fir, was used as an analgesic and antiseptic by Piscataqua tribes. Indians also collected the sap of the sugar maple for use as a cough syrup and expectorant, as well as a nutritious food. They used the hazelnut tree for skin ailments and fevers. Tea and poultices made of witch hazel treated numerous ailments, ranging from skin conditions, lung and intestinal problems to diseases of the eyes. Belknap, who listed the trees found along the Piscataqua Valley in volume three of the *History of New-Hampshire*, noted that the Indians used the American elm for kidney stones; walnut bark as a cathartic and for snakebite; the hemlock for intestinal complaints and as an astringent and analgesic; the ash as a snakebite antidote and for making baskets; Indian hemp for strings of the bow; lobelia (Indian tobacco) for an emetic and for bronchitis and asthma; buck bean for digestion and arthritis; and skunk cabbage for asthma.

The diet of the Indians of the Piscataqua Valley consisted of meat, fruits, nuts, vegetables and grains. If meat was not consumed soon after a kill, it was dried in the sun or smoked to make jerky. Wild fruits such as strawberries, plums, raspberries and blueberries were an important source of food in summer months. They also consumed acorns, walnuts and chestnuts. Roots and tubers, harvested wild or cultivated, included the groundnut and Jerusalem artichoke. Indian farmers cultivated melons, pumpkins, squash, beans and maize. Indians prepared land for cultivation by frequent burning to destroy underbrush and girdling, in which the cultivator stripped the bark from the lower trunk or made an incision around the trunk, which killed the tree and allowed sunlight to penetrate the soil the following year. Herring and shad caught in weirs, and placed in small mounds with seed, fertilized the soil for maize.

The tribes of the Piscataqua were small and under the influence of more powerful neighbors. To the east were the Abenaki, particularly the Norridgewocks of the Kennebec River Valley and the Penobscot tribe of the Penobscot Valley. According to John Smith, who in 1614 tried to precisely locate the varied tribes of the New England coast, the eastern tribes "hold the Bashabes of Pennobscot the chiefe and greatest amongst them." The chief (Bashabes) of the Penobscot tribe provided regional defense against a more feared tribe, the Tarratines (Micmacs) of New Brunswick and Nova Scotia. West of the Piscataqua tribes were the Penacooks of the Merrimack River Valley. Their chief, Passaconaway, was known for his power and wisdom throughout the region. The Penacooks provided defense against more powerful tribes to the west, such as the Mohawks. Neither the Tarratines nor the Mohawks, however, drove the Piscataqua, Squamscot and Newichawannock from the Piscataqua Valley; rather, it was the English.

CHAPTER TWO

LACONIA

While Martin Pring sailed the Atlantic and explored the coast and rivers of Maine and New Hampshire, other self-styled adventurers remained in England to plan and plot how they could grow rich from the efforts of Pring and other mariners. The death of Queen Elizabeth in 1603 and the accession of her nephew James, King of Scotland, brought about a new generation of courtiers intent on earning the king's favor. James, who was not afraid to make bold, if misinformed, decisions, responded to the appeal of numerous nobles, knights and gentlemen of London and Plymouth to grant them the right to settle the vast coast of North America. James responded in 1606, granting to two different groups of investors and adventurers—the London Company and the Plymouth Company—the rights to explore and colonize the region stretching from Georgia to Maine, which the English vaguely termed Virginia. The London Company was to settle the southern extent of Virginia and the Plymouth Company the northern extent. Both companies busily engaged themselves to send expeditions to their respective spheres of influence. The London Company sent a group of nobles, gentlemen and soldiers to South Virginia, where they landed, in 1607, on the James River, founding the colony of Jamestown.

Meanwhile the Plymouth Company organized an expedition under the sponsorship of Sir John Popham and Sir Ferdinando Gorges. Gorges was a soldier and commander of Plymouth Fort who had matured in the service of Elizabeth and retained, even after her death, the spirit of an adventurer intent on enlarging English power and his own personal wealth by founding and developing colonies in North America. He first became interested in New England in 1605 when, after George Weymouth had returned from a journey to the Penobscot Valley with five kidnapped Abenaki Indians, Gorges persuaded Weymouth to allow him to adopt three of the natives. Gorges got to know the three—Dehannida, Sketwarroes and Tarquantum—who informed Gorges about the bounty and beauty of northern New England. Teaming with Popham, Gorges sent two of the Indians on board the two ships that set sail for Maine and founded the short-lived Sagadahoc colony in 1607.

The colony foundered because of inadequate supplies, the unexpectedly harsh winter and the death of several leaders, including sponsor John Popham. Ferdinando Gorges, however, retained his interest in colonizing Northern Virginia. When John Smith returned from his brief voyage along the New England coast in 1614, Gorges was eager to engage his services in a colonizing venture to the Isles of Shoals and neighboring lands. Although Smith's attempts to return to New England never succeeded, Gorges sponsored the 1616 voyage of Richard Vines—a physician and veteran of Pring's 1603 voyage to the Piscataqua—along the New England coast, looking for a likely settlement. Vines found one at the mouth of the Saco River. He stayed the winter, then returned to England.

Gorges, excited by the prospects of a profitable fishing colony located near the Piscataqua Valley, joined with other nobles and merchants in requesting from King James the exclusive right to speculate and colonize this region, which John Smith had christened New England. In 1620 James granted a charter to the Council of New England. The two most energetic members of the council were Ferdinando Gorges and Captain John Mason, a merchant, soldier and former governor of Newfoundland. The council blindly granted patents of wilderness land about which they had no knowledge to adventurers, such as Gorges and Mason, who likewise were ignorant of the land they were so eager to exploit. In 1621 the council granted to Mason a grant of land (in present day Massachusetts) that ranged from the Naumkeag River to the Merrimack River; Mason, who had no idea what the patent entailed, called the grant Mariana. The next year the council granted to Mason and Gorges a patent between the Merrimack and Sagadahoc Rivers, extending inland an untold distance to the rivers and lakes of Canada. The two adventurers christened the grant Laconia. They considered it, in Belknap's words,

> *as a kind of terrestrial paradise, not merely capable of producing all the necessaries and conveniences of life but as already richly furnished by the bountiful hand of nature. The air was said to be pure and salubrious; the country pleasant and delightful, full of goodly forests, fair vallies, and fertile plains; abounding in vines, chestnuts, walnuts, and many other sorts of fruit; the rivers stored with fish and environed with goodly meadows full of timber trees.*

To settle Laconia and neighboring lands, and to establish the fishery and fur trades and make them profitable, the Council of New England, and sometimes individual members, sponsored explorers, settlers and agents. One of these adventurers, David Thomson, settled the mouth of the Piscataqua; another adventurer, Edward Hilton, settled Dover Point.

STRAWBERY BANKE

Scotsman David Thomson was an apothecary who journeyed to New England on several occasions, in 1606 as part of the Popham venture at Sagadahoc, and in 1616 accompanying his friend and associate Richard Vines to Saco River. Like many other apothecaries and physicians, Thomson was interested in the materia medica—flora useful as salves, analgesics and antiseptics—of the New England coast and inland rivers and forests. In 1621 he journeyed to the Piscataqua as an agent of the Council of New England. Supported by funding from several Plymouth merchants, Thomson and his "servants" sailed into the mouth of the Piscataqua in the ship *Jonathan*, anchoring at Little Harbor and establishing an initial settlement at Odiorne Point—a peninsula, almost an island at high tide, that juts into the mouth of the Piscataqua. From Odiorne Point the observer could scan the mouth of the Piscataqua, the distant Maine shore to the north and the Isles of Shoals lying a few miles to the east. Thomson fortified his settlement with a "Great House" as well as a fort with a palisade and small cannon. The settlers fished and hunted for sustenance, and explored the river, coast and islands.

The Council of New England subsequently granted a six-thousand-acre patent to Thomson that encompassed the whole of the Piscataqua Valley. Thomson called his patent Pannaway. According to a contemporary document written in 1660 by Samuel Maverick, who knew Thomson intimately, Thomson's plantation of Pannaway included "Strawberry Bank, The Great House & Isle of Shooles." Maverick's description continues:

> *Within 2 Myles of the Mouth is Strawberry Banke where are many Families, and a Minister & a Meeting House, and to the meeting Houses of Dower & Exceter, most of the people resort. This Strawberry Banke is part of 6000 acres granted by Patent about ye yeare 1620 or 1621, to Mr. David Thompson, who with the assistance of Mr. Nicholas Sherwill, Mr. Leonard Pomeroy and Mr. Abraham Colmer of Plymouth Merchants, went over with a Considerable Company of Servants and Built a Strong and Large House, enclosed it with a large and high Palizado and mounted Gunns, and being stored extraordinarily with shot and Ammunition was a Terror to the Indians, who at that time were insulting over the poor and weake and unfurnished Planters of Plymouth. This house and ffort he built on a Point of Land at the very entrance of Pasccatoway River. And having granted by Patent all the Island bordering on this land to the Midle of the River, he tooke possession of an Island comonly called the great Island and for the bounds of this side he went up the River to a point called Bloudy Point, and by the sea side about 4 miles he had also power of Government within his owne bounds. Notwithstanding all this, all is at this day in the power and at the disposall of the Massachusitts. Two Leagues out lyes the Isle of Shooles one of the best places for ffishing in the land, they have built a Church here and maintaine a Minister.*

Notwithstanding his patent, Thomson stayed at Pannaway only five years before relocating to an island in Boston Harbor. The inhabitants he left behind, unclear under what patent and whose authority they lived and worked, formed themselves into a body politic that at some point they designated "Strawbery Banke." The Council of New England, continuing to act in a confused and arbitrary fashion, granted several patents toward the end of the 1620s that apparently superseded earlier grants. John Mason received a patent in 1629 that included the "Pascataqua river, and up the same to the farthest head thereof." Mason, the governor of Hampshire in England, styled his new holding New Hampshire. Meanwhile the council granted another patent in 1630 for "all that part of the river Pascataqua called or known by the name of Hilton's Point" to Edward Hilton, who along with his brother William had set up a fishing operation at Dover Point beginning in 1623. The patent recognized the reality that the Hiltons had "at *their own* proper cost and charges, transported servants, built houses and planted corn." Hilton's patent, often called the Squamscot Patent, extended from the Piscataqua south to the Little Bay and Great Bay up the Squamscot River to the falls, where there was a new settlement called Exeter, the inhabitants of which had no reason or desire to respect Hilton or his patent. Adding to the confusion of this new realm of settlements and patents, the Council of New England granted another patent that included "that part of the patent of Laconia, on which the buildings and salt-work were erected, situate on both sides the harbor and river of Pascataqua to the extent of five miles westward by the sea-coast, then to cross over towards the other plantation in the hands of Edward Hilton." Multiple patents and confusion over what land belonged to whom led to sporadic conflict among the English. Bloody Point, which juts into the watery junction of the Piscataqua and Little Bay, was so named because settlers of the lower settlement at Strawbery Banke claimed the land at the same time as settlers at Dover Point. Whether blood was actually shed or merely contemplated is unclear.

John Mason and Ferdinando Gorges, attempting to wade through the muck of patents and possessions with their dignity and authority intact, sent a host of agents and servants in 1630 to make the declarations of the "adventurers" of the Council of New England a reality among the scattered inhabitants of the Piscataqua Valley. They appointed Captain Walter Neal the governor of the lower Piscataqua and Captain Thomas Wiggin governor of the upper valley. Captain Neal arrived to the Piscataqua in 1630 in the council's bark *Warwick*, establishing his base of operations at the Great House built by Thomson at Pannaway. His orders from the council were to establish a successful fishing operation, to supervise the growing settlements of the Piscataqua Valley, to inaugurate timber and fur trading industries and to explore the hinterland. Already the river and islands midstream and offshore were bustling with the activities of fishermen. The waters of the Gulf of Maine were alive with cod, haddock, flounder, sturgeon and herring. Fishermen sailing the Atlantic waters in small single-mast boats—the shallop— netted the fish and brought the catch back to shore, where they cleaned and split the fish, laying the fillets to dry in the sun or on wooden racks called flakes. Once dried, the fish were packed in barrels for export. The fishing business was particularly thriving at the Isles of Shoals and the Great Island (Newcastle) at the mouth of the river. Up and down the coast and upriver on both the northern and southern shores of the Piscataqua settlements were beginning and men planting fields and clearing the forests with which to build homes and boats; mills were erected to grind grain and to saw wood. Meanwhile the wives of the settlers established the semblance of normal home and town life.

Letters of the time record the difficulties the first Piscataqua settlers had adapting to the environment and making their venture profitable. Ambrose Gibbons was one of the men sent by the council to establish the fur trade with the native tribes and organize men to clear forests for shipments of timber to the Council of New England. He resided at Newichawannock, where the burgeoning trading and lumber settlement welcomed the local tribe for trade. Gibbons's house (or fort) was protected by a palisade and small arms. Even so Gibbons did not feel safe among the Newichawannock tribe, which he claimed were "far from neybors." Gibbons erected a sawmill and a gristmill, based on designs sent by the council, with the help of eight Danish laborers that Mason had sent. Gibbons tried planting grapevines with mixed success.

In time the place came to be called the Vineyard. Sarah Orne Jewett, in *The Old Town of Berwick*, described it almost three hundred years after Gibbons:

> *Everybody who has known the region since will remember the high, steep banks and green intervale below, shaded with fine elms and a magnificent hop hornbeam that stand apart or border the sheltered mill pond, entered on one side by the Great Works River and its wild gorge. The fall of water above, so famous in early history, is at least thirty feet in height, and rushes with great force past the cliffs; but below in the intervale it separates into brook-like streams, and flows gently among willows and alders, circling the mysterious Indian mound. Wild grapevines and tangles of clematis are festooned from tree to tree. In August the water brink is gay with cardinal flowers. Everything seems to grow in the Vineyard, and to bloom brighter than elsewhere…The shyest and rarest birds of the region may be seen there, in secret haunts, or at the time of their migration; it seems like Nature's own garden and pleasure ground. The old turf is like velvet, even on the high banks; and here grow great barberry-bushes, as they grow almost nowhere else. There is no doubt that they always mark for us the very oldest New England settlements and the site or neighborhood of old gardens. Brought over from England with other fruits and berries, they found a much more favorable soil and climate.*

Once Ambrose Gibbons had achieved some order in his surroundings at Newichawannock, the council sent, by the bark *Pide-Cow*, his wife and children. Trade with the Indians had netted seventy-six pounds of beaver pelts, ten otter pelts, six muskrat pelts and one martin pelt. Gibbons wrote that he wanted a mason to help with construction. The council wrote that it wanted to discover the mines of the region, and would send a soldier for the sake of the "discovrie" of said gold and silver. Responding to the council's complaints in a July 13, 1633, letter, Gibbons plainly wrote:

> *You complain of your returnes; you take the coorse to have little; a plantation must be furnished with cattle and good hir'd hands, and necessaries for them and not thinke the great lookes of men and many words will be a meanes to raise a plantation…For myself, my wife and child and four men we have but half a barrel of corne; beefe and porke I have not had…this three months, nor beare [beer] this four months; for I have for two and twenty months had but two barrels of beare and two barrels and four booshel of malt, our number commonly hath bin ten. I nor the servantes have neither money nor clothes.*

Captain Neal at Pannaway, meanwhile, worked for the council's interest at the lower Piscataqua. In the summer of 1633 he sent to the council 358 pounds of beaver and otter skins, seventeen martin skins, seventeen muskrat skins and several fox and raccoon skins. Even so he was under increasing pressure to send larger shipments of lumber and furs to England to make Laconia profitable. Neal determined to journey up the Piscataqua and explore its tributaries by birch canoe, then travel overland in the forests of southern Maine and eastern New Hampshire. The council was particularly concerned that Neal discover the great lakes—the most important being the Lake of the Iroquois—that they thought were to be found several days journey inland. The Lake of the Iroquois, the council believed, was near the "river of Canada"—to find a route from the Piscataqua to this great lake and river would ensure a successful fur trade with the Algonquin tribes of the interior. Neal set out in 1632 to discover the lake and river (Lake Champlain and the St. Lawrence River), ignorant of the distances involved. He reached Lake Winnipesaukee, which, though not the Lake of the Iroquois, was a significant and beautiful lake all the same. He then found his way barred by the White Mountains, which he explored but did not cross. Frustrated, the council recalled Neal in 1633 and put Francis Williams in charge of the lower plantation, which encompassed Strawbery Banke, Pannaway and the Great Island. On the northeast corner of the latter, guarding the harbor, was constructed the first of many forts, this one supplied with several cannon. Defenders of the plantation also had for their defense, "22 harquebusses, 4 muskets, 46 fowling pieces, 67 carbines, 6 pair of pistols, 61 swords and belts," and barrels of powder and bullets. For the maintenance of their fortifications, trade and fishery the colony had

> *375 yeards sail cloth, 12 bolts canvas…14 iron pots, 23 iron kettles, 1276 wrought pewter, 504 wrought brass, 5 barrels nails, 1 barrel spikes, 146 bars iron, 28 bars steel, quantities of all sorts of smith's cooper's carpenter's, mason's tools, 19 barrels of pitch, 16 barrels of tar, 8 coils of rope, of 1½ inches, 3 coils rope of 3½ inches, 10 cables of 4 inches, 12 herring nets, 6 seines, 70 cod lines, 67 mackerel lines, 11 gange cod hooks, 30 dozen mackerel hooks, 10 squid lines, 70 knots twine, 1500 boards, 1151 pine planks.*

In 1634 the Council of New England, frustrated by the lack of return for their investment, sold the interest in Laconia to Gorges and Mason, who divided their interests, Gorges taking the region from the Piscataqua north to Saco River (in Maine), and Mason keeping the region of the Piscataqua south (New Hampshire). Gorges sold to Mason the settlement at Newichawannock. Mason wrote Gibbons complaining of the money he had sunk into the venture without profit; Gibbons could only complain in his turn that the conception and supplying of Laconia was ill planned and insufficient from the outset. Indeed he was correct, as Gorges and Mason had from the beginning sought quick wealth in timber, fish, furs and precious stones, without a sure establishment of agriculture.

Strawbery Banke was the center of the vibrant Portsmouth merchant community from the 1600s to the 1800s. The site is now occupied by Strawbery Banke Museum. *Courtesy of Benjamin Lawson.*

The following year, Ferdinando Gorges determined finally to sail for New England to take actual possession of his plantation, which he had renamed New Somersetshire. His ship was made ready and the old knight boarded, bidding farewell to England—or so he thought: the ship foundered before it left Plymouth harbor, and Gorges resigned himself to staying in England, never to venture to America. Captain John Mason, meanwhile, prepared to invest more resources to make Laconia, now renamed New Hampshire, profitable. "But death," Belknap wrote, "which puts an end to the fairest prospects, cut off all the hopes which Mason had entertained of aggrandizing his fortune, by the settlement of New-Hampshire."

SELF-GOVERNMENT

Mason's death forced the burgeoning communities of Strawbery Banke at the lower Piscataqua and Dover and Newichawannock at the upper Piscataqua to fend for themselves in the way of self-government. As the men and women of the Piscataqua Valley were English, they brought to America English traditions of local government. They formed compacts of self-government based on the decisions of the male citizens in assembly. Issues of property and religion were paramount in the minds of the citizens. The citizens of Strawbery Banke, for example, in 1640 decided to set aside "glebe" land for a church and parsonage, which was in accord with English tradition. The document granting the glebe land states:

> *Whereas divers and sundry of the Inhabitants of the Lower end of Pascataquack…of their free and voluntary mind, good wills and assents, without constraint or compulsion of any manner of person or persons, have granted, given and contributed divers and several sums of money towards the building, erecting, and founding of a parsonage house, with a chapel thereto united as also fiftie acres of Glebe land which is annexed and given to the said parsonage….Now the said Inhabitants aforesaid by their common assent and consent toward the furtherance and advancement of the honor and glory of God, doe give, grant, aliene and set over unto Thomas Walford and Henry Sherburne, Church Wardens of this Parish…all the said Parsonage house, chappell, cornfield, garden glebe land with the appurtenances, with all our right, title, interest in and to the sayd premises to remane, endure and continue in perpetuitie for ever to the use of the aforesaid parish.*

The citizens of other towns and settlements in the Piscataqua Valley at the same time began to take matters of self-government into their own hands. The majority of the citizens of Dover resided at Hilton's Point, where they had constructed a meetinghouse. In 1640 the inhabitants formed themselves into a body politic, pledging their loyalty to the government of England. Residents at Newichawannock, meanwhile, under the leadership of Humphrey Chadbourne (Ambrose Gibbons having relocated to Great Island), continued the cutting of trees and making of boards as the principal concern of the settlement. Chadbourne purchased a large tract of land along the Great Works

River from the local Indian sachem Rowls and was a leading citizen at a time, after the death of Mason, when there was a vacuum in outside leadership. Chadbourne later relocated to Kittery, after that town had assumed the leading role among all the scattered settlements of the northern shores of the Piscataqua.

The settlers at the falls of the Squamscot River, meanwhile, formed themselves into a body politic called Exeter. The founder of Exeter was John Wheelwright, the brother of Anne Hutchinson, who had caused turmoil at Massachusetts Bay over her rejection of community authority for personal authority in spiritual matters. Hutchinson was banished south to Rhode Island. Wheelwright, joined by his followers, migrated north to the falls of the Squamscot River, which was inhabited by the Squamscot tribe. What happened in the interaction between the English and Indians remains a mystery. Whether Wheelwright forged a relationship of goodwill, intimidated the Indians into submitting to the English or purchased the land from the Indians is unknown. Before the early nineteenth century, it was thought by such historians as Jeremy Belknap that Wheelwright purchased the land from the native inhabitants. But scholars and antiquarians during the 1800s disputed the legitimacy of the Wheelwright Deed, branding it a forgery. All the same, in August 1639, the inhabitants of Exeter agreed upon the following "combination":

The imposing granite walls of the military fortress on Kittery Point. *Courtesy of Benjamin Lawson.*

We…brethren of the church in Exeter, situate and lying upon the river Pascataqua, with other inhabitants there, considering with ourselves the holy will of God and our own necessity, that we should not live without wholesome laws and civil government among us, of which we are altogether destitute, do in the name of Christ and in the sight of God combine ourselves together to erect and set up among us such government as shall be to our best discerning agreeable to the will of God, professing ourselves subjects of our Sovereign Lord King Charles, according to the liberties of our English colony of Massachusetts, and binding of ourselves solemnly by the grace and help of Christ, and in his name and fear, to submit ourselves to such godly and christian laws as are established in the realm of England to our best knowledge, and to all other such laws which shall upon good grounds be made and enacted among us according to God, that we may live quietly [and] *peaceably together in all godliness and honesty.*

In 1641 the Council of New England had been defunct and Mason had been dead for several years, and the political controversy in England between the king and Parliament was leading to an increasingly volatile situation (which would in time result in civil war). The towns of the Piscataqua Valley—Strawbery Banke, Kittery, Dover, Exeter and Hampton—jointly determined to put themselves under the protection of their stronger neighbor to the south. They mutually pledged allegiance to Massachusetts Bay on the condition that their local affairs would continue to be managed as before, and that suffrage and political office would not be dependent upon membership in a congregational church, as was current in Massachusetts.

The leaders of Massachusetts, such as John Winthrop, had long coveted control over the lands between the Merrimack and Piscataqua Rivers and beyond to the north, and they interpreted their own charter to include these lands. Massachusetts incorporated the Piscataqua towns into the new county of Norfolk. The shire town or seat of the county was Salisbury in Massachusetts, but court sessions were held in Dover and Portsmouth as well. These two towns were sufficiently large to send delegates to the Massachusetts legislature, the General Court. The Dover representative in 1644, for example, was William Hilton, who along with his brother Edward had been the original settlers of Dover.

Massachusetts Bay had been founded in 1630 as, in Winthrop's words, "a city upon a hill," a New Jerusalem where the Puritans would carry out the role of God's chosen on this divine "errand into the wilderness." Although Puritans in theory believed that each individual had the freedom to read and interpret the scripture, in practice social and political order required conformity to a set belief—Calvinism. The Puritans believed it was their calling to spread their Calvinist beliefs throughout America. The merchants, fishermen, shipbuilders and sawyers of the Piscataqua, however, were reluctant to subscribe to religious conformity. They agreed with the Massachusetts Puritans that Roman Catholicism, such as that practiced by France and its colony in Canada, was in error, but there were many Piscataqua residents that had been perfectly content with the Church of England (the Anglican Church) and saw no reason to depart from it. Piscataqua towns such as Portsmouth, therefore, developed a thriving Anglican community.

THE MASON CONTROVERSY

Meanwhile, the political status of Newichawannock remained uncertain, as it was not part of the county of Norfolk and not clearly within the jurisdiction of Massachusetts. Newichawannock had been part of Mason's holdings, and though he had died in 1636, his heir Robert Tufton, who took the surname Mason, sued for control of his grandfather John Mason's original proprietorship. The government of Massachusetts, wary of such proprietary claims and unwilling to limit its growing power and authority, determined to gain an accurate assessment of the lands it was legitimately entitled to control. Amid the confusing patents issued by the Council of New England in the 1620s and 1630s was one that declared that the boundaries of Massachusetts extended to three miles north of the Merrimack River and all land contained therein. In 1652 Massachusetts Bay, seeking to make the most of such vague determinations, sent two explorer-surveyors to ascend the Merrimack River to its source. John Sherman and Jonathan Ince reached the supposed source of the Merrimack at Lake Winnipesaukee at latitude "fourty three degrees, fourty minutes and twelve seconds" north. Simultaneously, Massachusetts sent a ship to determine where along the coast of Maine was the same latitude. Jonas Clarke and Samuel Andrews found that forty-three degrees, forty minutes and twelve seconds fell at the northern end of Casco Bay. Massachusetts therefore claimed all of the lands extending from Lake Winnipesaukee to Casco Bay, which encompassed most of the patents of Mason and Gorges.

The controversy with Robert Tufton Mason continued for decades, particularly after 1660, when Charles II became king after the failed English Commonwealth under Oliver Cromwell. Mason was a firm supporter of Charles, who disliked the independence and power of Massachusetts Bay and gave the proprietor as much support as he could. Charles appointed a royal commission in 1664 to travel to New England and to investigate and report on the government of Massachusetts. The commissioners were highhanded, encouraging the Piscataqua Valley towns to join together and secede from the government of Massachusetts. The Piscataqua towns refused to abandon Massachusetts, yet also knew that their best interests lay in accommodating the demands of the king. In 1666, for example, because of war with the Dutch, in response to the king's request as conveyed by the royal commissioners to fortify the mouth of the Piscataqua, Portsmouth, Kittery and Dover joined together to erect a fort on Great Island. It was determined that "the neck of land on the eastward of the Great Island, where a small fort had been already built," would be "sequestered for the purpose." The old fort had earthen walls and four small cannon; the expansion involved the erection of a wooden blockhouse. According to Belknap, "the customs and imposts on goods imported into the harbor were applied to the maintenance of the fort, and the trained [militia] bands of Great-Island and Kittery-Point were discharged from all other duty to attend the service of it, under Richard Cutt, esquire, who was appointed captain."

The powder house at Fort McClary held munitions for artillery during the early years of the 1800s. *Courtesy of Benjamin Lawson.*

Fort Constitution defended the entrance to the Piscataqua before the Revolution as Fort William and Mary. *Photo by the author.*

PORTSMOUTH

Charles II established New Hampshire as a royal province in 1679, partly to limit Massachusetts's influence, partly to address the demands of Mason and partly because the Piscataqua towns were becoming wealthy and stable, able to exist independently. The dominant town was Portsmouth. The town records, which begin in 1652, describe a well-ordered and governed town. The assembly of all male citizens regularly met and voted on town officers and made decisions respecting taxation, property, the poor and the particular affairs of inhabitants. Portsmouth, like all of the Piscataqua towns, gave the power of daily governance to the "select" men; the assembly voted in April 1652 to empower the selectmen to act "as though our selves the wholl Towne wear Present"— though "the Power, Remains to the wholl Towne."

Some of the activities of the selectmen included setting tax rates and determining the allotment of land to new inhabitants. Initially, newcomers received eight acres of land provided that they passed social and economic muster—it was up to the selectmen to determine whether or not the newcomer was of a sufficient status and wealth to be accepted as a legal landowning inhabitant. In September 1653, the assembly voted on a clerk of the market, charged with regulating the buying and selling of goods according to accepted practices and prices. In March 1654, the town selected two constables to keep the peace and collect taxes. In April, the town voted to assign seats in the meetinghouse according to wealth and rank—merchants and landowners sat in the front, and successive rows went to craftsmen, shopkeepers, farmers and laborers. Selectmen had to carefully make such assignments, as an inhabitant's personal pride and self-perception of rank could easily lead to controversy. Hence, selectman John Pickering was called before the town in 1659 to answer to misdemeanor charges of slighting an important citizen by assigning a seat in the meetinghouse not befitting the great man's rank.

Families did not sit together in the meetinghouse; women were given a separate place to sit, and children were situated as far as possible from the pulpit so as not to disturb the minister's contemplative remarks. The town appointed an inhabitant whose sole job on the Sabbath was to "look after the demeanoer of the boyes at meeting." In March 1655, the assembly selected three men to oversee the construction of a parsonage on the glebe land, which was fifty acres set aside for the purposes of the church. Portsmouth continued to resist the spiritual influence of Massachusetts Puritanism, often supporting Anglican ministers, which was wholly proper for an English colony. Nevertheless, Puritan strictness exercised some influence over the town. For example, in 1662 the assembly voted that any inhabitant found sleeping or smoking on the Sabbath would be fined.

At Portsmouth, like other Piscataqua Valley towns, the assembly of citizens kept strict control over all town affairs. Owners of taverns (ordinaries) had to receive permission to set up business. Talking out of turn and other such disruptions in town meetings resulted in a stiff fine for the malefactor. Anyone who refused to serve in a town office was fined as well. Befitting an image of an orderly godly community, any disruption or conflict was nipped in the bud. Officials were appointed to survey lands, negotiate boundaries between Portsmouth and other towns and represent Portsmouth at the Massachusetts

General Court. The fence viewer settled disputes between inhabitants regarding property boundaries. The hog reeve kept the town pen and corralled disruptive hogs. All inhabitants, on pain of a fine, were required to pay a tax to support the minister.

It was, of course, inevitable that some inhabitants would be unable to pay the parish rate, or properly care for themselves in other ways. Portsmouth like other growing New England towns sought "to Keepe the Town harmless from being burthened in way of Charge" of caring for inhabitants who could not care for themselves. Portsmouth adopted the practice of "warning out" those who were newcomers to the town but who could not give proof of their financial stability either by the purchase of property or the visible possession of sufficient wealth. Hence, in 1671 the town constable informed Henry Russell that he must leave the town; otherwise if he was ever unable to care for himself, the town would refuse material aid. Russell, however, argued his case before the selectmen, convincing them that he would not become a charge, so was allowed to stay. In February 1679, the selectmen warned John Davis from town "for better security to save the Towne from charge." Until he and his wife departed, the town provided corn and meat for her sustenance. Townspeople who welcomed strangers, friends or family members to their homes were frequently admonished by the selectmen and ordered "to give an account of there being in Town, and for Having entertaining of strangers without Liberty." In July 1686, John Kelly, who had initially settled in Portsmouth then later brought his wife and two children to live with him, "was warned by the Selectmen to give securety, for saveing the Town from any charge of himself and wife and children or to depart."

Jackson House, Portsmouth. This early twentieth-century print is of the oldest house in the Piscataqua Valley, constructed in 1664. *From* Vignettes of Portsmouth.

The people of Portsmouth were not inhumane, merely careful to avoid having the burden of caring for what the English called the "sturdy beggar." The helpless and infirm, particularly those of longstanding residence, were cared for without complaint. In June 1678, "Jennets orphan child," who was five years old, was bound to Samuel Haynes "to find her with sufficient meate, drinke, clothing washing and Lodging and to teach her to reade for all which said term wee the Selectmen bind her to him." Haynes was paid twenty pounds. During the 1690s the town repeatedly paid inhabitants to care for "Father Lewes," who was very old and unable to care for himself. Lewes had been one of Mason's men who came to the Piscataqua Valley in the 1630s.

THE PROVINCE OF NEW HAMPSHIRE

The new royal province of New Hampshire was established in 1679, under the presidency of John Cutt, who chose for his council leading men of the Piscataqua Valley towns, such as Richard Waldron of Dover and John Gilman of Exeter. Waldron was appointed commander of the provincial militia. Courts of justice were established and laws passed. Only property-owning males could vote, which in 1680 totaled seventy-one in Portsmouth, sixty-one in Dover and twenty in Exeter. Capital laws of the province included the death penalty for blasphemy by worshiping gods other than the Christian god or by denying the Christian Trinity; for treason, rebellion and murder; for "carnal copulation" with "a brute creature"; for "any man" who "lieth with mankind as he lieth with a woman"; for arson and rape; for children (over the age of sixteen) who showed violence toward or otherwise wantonly disobeyed parents; and for witchcraft (a person who "hath or consulteth with a familiar spirit"). That this was a credulous age is illustrated by the proclamation of the president and council in March 1681 of a fast,

> upon serious consideration of the manifold sinful provocations among us, as of the sundry tokens of divine displeasure evident to us, both in the present dangerous sickness of the honorable president of the council of New-Hampshire, in the continuance of whose life is wrapt up much blessing, whose death may occasion much trouble; as also in respect of that awful portentous blazing star, usually foreboding sore calamity to the beholders thereof.

Notwithstanding the fast, President John Cutt died soon after. The "blazing star" was also observed by scientists of Boston, such as Increase and Cotton Mather, who knew it as the comet of 1680.

Robert Tufton Mason, the loyal sycophant of King Charles, convinced the king that his claim of proprietor of the province was valid and promised the king portions of the rents he would charge the inhabitants should he be given the authority to carry out the scheme. The king was agreeable and Mason, unwilling to himself force the issue upon the inhabitants of the Piscataqua, achieved the appointment of a royal governor friendly to his interests, Edward Cranfield, who arrived at Portsmouth in 1682.

Cranfield, during his brief administration, imposed rules upon the local churches and taxes upon the people. Attempting at first to obtain the assistance of the assembly in his designs, Cranfield was frustrated by the refusal of the members of the assembly to cooperate with him to negate the liberty and independence of self-government that the colony had hitherto enjoyed. The Piscataqua Valley as a whole refused to cooperate with the governor, who eventually was removed from office, but not before two years of oppression. Cranfield removed the leading men, such as Richard Waldron and William Vaughan, from the council, replacing them with his cronies, such as Walter Barefoote and Edward Randolph. Mason, who also had a seat on the council, began a series of lawsuits against landowners to recoup his losses as proprietor. Waldron and Vaughan, as well as other leading Piscataqua merchants and landowners, were brought to court; some, such as Vaughan, were committed to prison for disobedience and recalcitrance.

The minister of the first parish, Joshua Moody, was also imprisoned after challenging the governor's authority. Cranfield laid a trap for Moody, demanding of the congregational clergyman that he administer the sacrament of the Eucharist in accord with the Church of England, the state religion of England. Moody, who was not ordained an Anglican priest, naturally refused, whereupon he was brought to trial and committed to prison. Vaughan, in a long epistle that he wrote of his experiences, described in detail the haughty behavior of Cranfield and Mason, how they confiscated property and money for rents and taxes in a brazen attempt to enrich themselves, how they arbitrarily committed people to prison on trumped up charges, and no one—male or female, young or old—was safe from their deprecations. Belknap, writing at the time of the American Revolution, saw in the response of the Piscataqua patriots of 1684 a similar response to the Patriots of 1776. "In a country where the love of liberty had ever been the ruling passion," he wrote,

> it could not be expected but that some forward spirits would break the restraints of prudence, and take a summary method to put a stop to their oppressions. Several persons had declared that they would sooner part with their lives, than suffer distraints; and associations were formed for mutual support. At Exeter, the sheriff was resisted and driven off with clubs; the women having prepared hot spits and scalding water to assist in the opposition.

Eventually, such disorder along with complaints and petitions made to the king (by means of Portsmouth agent Nathaniel Weare, in London) forced Cranfield to give up his post and flee the province.

The death of King Charles II and ascension of King James II in 1685 occasioned yet another new form of government, the Dominion of New England, which included the former independent colonies of Massachusetts Bay, including Maine, Plymouth and New Hampshire. Governing the Dominion was Edmund Andros, who imposed an administration in which, in the words of Belknap, "the press was restrained; liberty of conscience infringed; exorbitant fees and taxes demanded, without the voice or consent of the people, who had no privilege of representation."

Once known as the Old South Meetinghouse, housing the first parish of Portsmouth, this building is today used for the Portsmouth Children's Museum. *Courtesy of Benjamin Lawson.*

James's reign was, however, short-lived; the Parliament deposed the king and, in the Glorious Revolution of 1689, offered the crown to William of Orange, contingent upon his agreement that monarchal rule be tempered by the rule of law and respect for the rights of English men and women. Even so, and although the Dominion of New England was suspended, during the reign of King William, then Queen Anne, New Hampshire continued to be governed by an assortment of mediocre governors who rarely represented the interests of the people. The concern that Piscataqua residents had over the many confusing changes in government were, however, secondary to an even greater threat to their lives and liberty—King William's War.

CHAPTER THREE

A CENTURY OF CONFLICT

The English settled the Piscataqua Valley during a time when Europeans were hungry for land, riches and power. North America in particular represented a vast unknown that could be settled and exploited by humans with tireless courage and will. The treasures of America, both real and imagined, spurred adventurers and settlers across the Atlantic, up rivers and over mountains. The Spanish were first to penetrate North America; explorers and conquistadors such as Hernando de Soto and Francisco Coronado journeyed and fought their way through the southeast Gulf region, the southwest deserts and up the western coast. French explorers such as Jacques Cartier, Samuel de Champlain, Jacques Marquette and Louis Jolliet, René Robert, Sieur de La Salle, Pierre and Paul Mallet, Bénard de La Harpe and Étienne Veniard de Bourgmont journeyed along the eastern coast, up the St. Lawrence River, throughout the Great Lakes, down the Mississippi River and up the rivers of the Great Plains to the Rocky Mountains. English explorers such as John Smith, Henry Hudson, Darby Field and John Lederer, ascending the rivers of the East Coast—the Penobscot, Hudson, Connecticut, Susquehanna and James—to the foothills of the Appalachians, forged paths that settlers subsequently took. The competition for control of America mirrored the competition among European powers, particularly the Spanish, French, Dutch and English, for control of Europe. Indian tribes such as the Abenaki found themselves in between the French and English rivalry in northern New England. Frequently the conflict of the French, Indians and English descended upon the towns of the Piscataqua Valley.

That the Indians of New England sided with the French rather than the English in the wars of the seventeenth and eighteenth centuries is explained in part by the actions of English settlers during the middle decades of the 1600s. The Penobscot, Piscataqua, Squamscot, Newichawannock and Abenaki tribes had their forests and rivers in which they hunted and fished overtaken by an increasing population of English settlers who, unlike the Indians, did not gently use the land and its resources. Rather, they exploited the forests and rivers for the wealth in furs, timber, power and fish contained therein. The English "purchased" the lands of the Indians either by guile or subterfuge, the unwitting natives discovering in time that the English conception of ownership meant the private possession of lands and waters and the corollary concept of trespass— traditional hunting and fishing spots as well as camps along the falls of rivers were no longer available to the Indians. Finding, therefore, the traditional means of livelihood limited by the English, the Indians relocated inland to find forests with game and streams with fish—but the expansion of English settlement always appeared close behind. The inexorable movement of the English resulted in resentment among the Indian tribes, who often lashed out in frustration and revenge. The first such occasion occurred in the 1670s during King Philip's War.

A "WOODEN" WORLD

Although King Philip's War began in Massachusetts, it unsettled all of New England and inspired some Indians who nursed a grudge or saw an opportunity to rid the land of the English to make sporadic attacks at the Piscataqua Valley. The outlying towns of the Piscataqua, situated on the falls of the tributaries of the Piscataqua, were built on the surrounding northern forest. Exeter, Dover and Newichawannock were mill towns, where the inhabitants in one way or another made their living from the forest. Men worked in teams going deep into the forest with axes, adzes, chains, wagons and draft animals to fell and drag the choicest offerings of the forest. The Piscataqua basin featured a cornucopia of hard and soft woods. Shipwrights of Piscataqua towns erected shipyards on the main riverbanks of the Piscataqua, Newichawannock, Cocheco and Squamscot, or even upstream nearer the forests. Piscataqua shipbuilders constructed fishing shallops fitted with a single mast and sail and open hull; barks and ketches with two masts and sails and an enclosed hull; the pinnace, used for coastal trade, with three masts; and the ship, the largest boat made, which could hold up to one hundred tons. Shipwrights oversaw the use of black oak for ship keels and ribs, white pine for masts, yellow pine for ship decking, locust for wooden pegs to join ribs to keel and beam and white ash for oars. Sawyers cut the wood, caulkers used oakum to caulk the seams of the boat, joiners did carpentry work, sailmakers used esoteric tools exclusive to their craft and ropemakers made rope from hemp.

By the late 1600s, the white pine was already sought after by shipwrights in America and England for its height and straightness, perfect for masts, yards and bowsprits of ships. These pines soared one hundred feet to the ceiling of the New England forest. They were two to three feet in diameter and could withstand the lashing gales of the Atlantic. In time, during the seventeenth and eighteenth centuries, the English Crown assumed the right to reserve the best white pines for the British navy, and surveyors tramped through the northern New England forest, even those privately owned, marking out pines reserved exclusively for the use of the king. It was difficult yet delicate work to fell and preserve a mast pine. Belknap, who lived in Dover and knew the particulars of harvesting the mast pine, described the process in the third volume of the *History of New-Hampshire*:

When a mast tree is to be felled, much preparation is necessary. So tall a stick without any limbs nearer the ground than eighty or a hundred feet, is in great danger of breaking in the fall. To prevent this, the workmen have a contrivance which they call bedding the tree, which is thus executed. They know in what direction the tree will fall; and they cut down a number of small trees which grow in that direction; or if there be none, they draw others to the spot, and place them so that the falling tree may lodge on their branches, which breaking or yielding under its pressure, render its fall easy and safe. A time of deep snow is the most favorable season, as the rocks are then covered, and a natural bed is formed to receive the tree. When fallen, it is examined, and if to appearance it be sound, it is cut in the proportion of three feet in length to every inch of its diameter, for a mast.

To retrieve the tree from the forest and deliver it to the shipwrights required similarly great effort. Axe-men prepared a path through the forest, cutting a primitive road from the white pine stand to the nearest stream or river. Teams of oxen hitched to chains pulled the big sticks (as they were called) through the forest. In winter, massive sleds were used to slide the tree along a declivity to the waiting stream, where the masts-to-be waited the spring thaw before being conveyed to the falls of the Squamscot or Cocheco. The best mast pines were loaded aboard vessels bound for England. "Those of inferior size," Belknap wrote, "partly unsound, crooked, or broken in falling, are either sawn into planks and boards, or formed into canoes, or cut into bolts for the use of coopers, or split and shaved into clapboards and shingles" for Piscataqua homes. Pine trees also yielded important naval stores, such as tar and turpentine. Tar was collected by locating a clay deposit around which a trench was dug. Pine logs were formed in a conical fashion at the center of the clay and covered with earth. Workers lit a fire in the middle of the cone, which smoldered, releasing the dark liquid, which then flowed into the trench, where it was collected in barrels. Turpentine flowed from incisions made in white pines.

Sawmills were erected upon first settlement at the falls of the Squamscot, Cocheco and Newichawannock Rivers. The easiest design was a horizontal wheel, turned by the power of the water, which drove a belt powering the saw. Sawyers and carpenters used wood from numerous trees for a variety of domestic purposes. Pine afforded excellent wood for flooring and clapboard. Spruce and hemlock were used in building houses, barns, bridges and fences. Carpenters used the wood of aspen, elm, cherry, sassafras and maple for furniture. Barrel staves were made from oak, wagon wheels from elm and gunstocks from walnut. The sugar maple was chiefly used to produce maple sugar and syrup. Farmers made an incision near the base of the tree in March, when winter thawing began. The sap flowed best on sunny days. Farmers collected the sap in buckets hung from the trees, which were emptied into larger trowels. When sufficient sap was collected, it was put in large caldrons and boiled over open fires until the sap turned to a thick syrup or boiled down to a sweet crystal.

During the colonial period, most Piscataqua residents were farmers. Although the inhabitants of Portsmouth in 1653 complained in a letter to the Massachusetts General Court that "the quality of the land we live on is so bad, it's incredible to believe, except those which have seen it," some soils of the Piscataqua yielded good crops. The frequent freshets of spring resulted in rich and fertile intervale land in the river valleys. Experienced husbandmen could determine the quality of farmland depending on forest growth. White pine, beech, maple, birch and red oak indicated rich soil that could support most crops. Pitch pine, hemlock, spruce and white oak land possessed soil that was thin and sandy or rocky, requiring tremendous labor to produce crops such as maize. Belknap learned from the husbandmen of the Piscataqua that the best time to clear the land of trees was June, when the days are longest and farmers had already (in May) sown the seed. The following year, in mid-spring, the farmer burned the dry felled trees when the soil was moist. Because of the plentiful stones, trunks and roots left in the soil, farmers sometimes plowed, but just as often used a hoe to dig small holes in which to drop the seed. Preferred crops were maize, barley, rye and wheat. In early autumn at harvest time, townspeople gathered together in celebration, husking corn, eating and dancing. Farmers encouraged the growth of fruit trees, especially apples, and cider was the preferred drink among all ages. Cattle, hogs, goats and sheep of Piscataqua farms descended from those originally brought to Laconia in the 1630s.

King Philip's War

On such towns of the Piscataqua, Algonquian warriors descended in September 1675. The first place attacked were farms along the Oyster River, one of the tributaries of the Great Bay, situated southwest of Dover and originally part of that township. The first inhabitants of Oyster River arrived in the 1630s, and farmed the rich valley land and grazed livestock on the plentiful marsh grass. Oyster River was tidal below the falls, and farmers shipped their goods down the river by small boats, barges or shallops to the larger port at Portsmouth. The Indians attacked and burned half a dozen Oyster River houses and killed several men. Another band of warriors attacked Newichawannock around the same time. They cornered fifteen women and children in a fortified house. Save for the heroism of an eighteen-year-old woman, who barricaded the door while the others escaped, they would have all been killed or captured. The Indian attacks brought "fear and confusion" to "all the plantations at Pascataqua," Belknap wrote:

> *Business was suspended, and every man was obliged to provide for his own and his family's safety. The only way was to desert their habitations, and retire together within the larger and more convenient houses, which they fortified with a timber wall and flankarts, placing a sentry-box on the roof. Thus the labor of the field was exchanged for the duty of the garrison, and they, who had long lived in peace and security, were upon their guard night and day, subject to continual alarms, and the most fearful apprehensions.*

The Piscataqua towns mustered the militia in response to the attacks. Towns required every able-bodied man over the age of sixteen and under the age of fifty to muster on the town green at infrequent times to stand in formation and engage in drills under the commanding officer, usually a captain. Every man, of course, owned a musket, powder and balls, typically employed to put meat on the family table, but also to bear arms for the defense of their families and property. During times of emergency, the militia of the several towns mustered under the command of a regional commander, which in this case was Major Richard Waldron of Dover. In addition to town militia, Waldron also commanded one troop of cavalry and a company of artillery that mustered for service at the fort on Great Island. Waldron was the leading citizen of Dover, having emigrated from England in 1640, when he was twenty-five years old. From 1654 to 1679, he represented Dover in the Massachusetts General Court, the provincial legislature, serving as speaker for seven of those years. When New Hampshire became an independent colony in 1679, Waldron served on the provincial council and was for several years president of the province.

Upon the death of King Philip in 1676, the war drew to a close. Regional tribes of the Piscataqua and Merrimack came to Dover to make peace, negotiating with Major Waldron. Some of the tribes, such as the Penacook under Wonolanset, had not engaged in hostilities during the war; but others, Indians from Massachusetts that Piscataqua locals designated the "strange" Indians, had fled to the north and tried to mix with the more peaceful tribes. They were discovered, however, in the following way: According to Belknap, four hundred Indians arrived at Dover to treat with Major Waldron, who embraced them in friendship. Several militia captains, however, informed him of the presence of the renegade "strange" Indians, and Waldron formed a plan to capture them. He invited the four hundred warriors to join the militia in training, including "a sham fight after the English mode." The Indians faced the colonials and were bade to fire their weapons first, whereupon the militia surrounded them, separated the "strange" Indians from the rest and sent them under guard to Boston, where some were executed. However, the majority was sold into slavery abroad.

Those Indians allowed to go free, as can be imagined, believed Major Waldron to be duplicitous; indeed, the action, rather than bringing peace, merely inspired the Indians to engage in further hostilities. Besides this mistake, the colonials erred in inviting the Mohawks of New York to send a force to northern New England to make war on their inveterate enemies, the Abenaki. The Mohawks made war, however, not only on the aggressors among the Indians, but also the peaceful, which angered the tribes of northern New England, convincing them that the English could no longer be trusted. Various sachems, such as Mogg and Squando, led the Abenaki warriors in continued depredations on the settlements along the Maine coast, Kittery and Portsmouth. Waldron and other militia leaders marched north on several occasions to find and destroy the attackers, with limited success. Eventually the governor of New York Edmund Andros sent forces to build a fort at Pemaquid on the coast of Maine. This, combined with a party of negotiators from Piscataqua, led to a peace treaty in 1678, ending hostilities after three years.

KING WILLIAM'S WAR

Peace blessed the Piscataqua for a decade before war once again came to the region, this time as part of a larger European war, which colonials called King William's War. The first Piscataqua community to experience bloodshed was Dover. Situated at the Cocheco Falls, the settlement of Dover was in 1689 limited to five garrisoned houses, one of which was Major Waldron's. These garrisons were particularly well made with large beams, thick wooden walls and iron bolts. Such preventative construction, however, did not avail Major Waldron on one particular evening in June 1689. The local Abenaki frequently visited the garrison, trading and mingling, eating supper, even sleeping by the fireplace. Some Dover residents were apprehensive of such familiarity. "When," according to Belknap, "some of the people hinted their fears" to Major Waldron, "he merrily bade them to go and plant their pumpkins, saying that he would tell them when the Indians would break out." On the night of June 27, however, the Indians acted upon a preconcerted plan, in which they surrounded the Waldron garrison and broke into the major's room while he was asleep. The major, Belknap wrote,

> *awakened by the noise…jumped out of bed, and though now advanced in life to the age of eighty years, he retained so much vigor as to drive them with his sword, through two or three doors; but as he was returning for his other arms, they came behind him, stunned him with a hatchet, drew him into his hall, and seating him in an elbow chair, on a long table, insultingly asked him, "Who shall judge Indians now?" They then obliged the people in the house to get them some victuals; and when they had done eating, they cut the major across the breast and belly with knives, each one with a stroke, saying, "I cross out my account." They then cut off his nose and ears, forcing them into his mouth; and when spent with the loss of blood, he was falling down from the table, one of them held his own sword under him, which put an end to his misery.*

Besides Waldron's garrison, the Otis and Coffin garrisons—which had been specifically fortified with eight-foot-high, twelve-inch-thick walls—were destroyed. Waldron was one of twenty-three inhabitants killed by the raiders. Richard Otis, whose house was a focal point of local defense, died along with a son and daughter. His wife was among twenty-nine taken from Dover and brought to Canada and auctioned as slaves to the highest French bidder. One of Major Waldron's granddaughters, Sarah Gerrish, was seven years old when she was kidnapped and taken to Canada, where she was eventually put in a convent, unable to return to New England for nine years. Other Piscataqua Valley settlements were similarly attacked. At Salmon Falls, in March 1690, fifty-two raiders attacked and killed thirty defenders and kidnapped fifty-four women and children. Among those captured was Mehetable Goodwin, who was separated from her husband and forced to march north with her newborn baby, who was killed because it encumbered the march. Goodwin supposed her husband dead, and after a time in Quebec remarried a Canadian and bore several children. Eventually she returned to the Piscataqua to live out her life with her first husband.

During the spring of 1690, settlements at Fox Point at Newington, the Lamprey River and Exeter were also attacked, the people suffering heavy casualties. During the summer, French and Indian attackers killed upwards of forty people. Piscataqua militia led by local officers went in pursuit of the raiders, with mixed success. During these several years, according to Belknap,

> *the people of New-Hampshire were much reduced; their lumber trade and husbandry being greatly impeded by the war. Frequent complaints were made of the burden of the war, the scarcity of provisions, and the dispiritedness of the people…The governor was obliged to impress men to guard the outposts: they were sometimes dismissed for want of provisions, and then the garrison officers were called to account and severely punished… The towns of Dover and Exeter being more exposed than Portsmouth or Hampton, suffered the greatest share in the common calamity. Nothing but the hope of better times kept alive their fortitude.*

There was a short respite from war, a brief cease-fire followed by a resumption of attacks in the summer of 1694, this time of greater ferocity. Over several hundred French and Indian warriors overwhelmed the Oyster River settlement. Oyster River below the falls, in the present town of Durham, rises and falls with the tide, the air sometimes tinged with salt and the land low, wet and marshy. The population of farm families lived along the river and its tributaries. Orchards dotted the land, the fruit growing large. Marsh grasses awaited the scythe. The inhabitants had prepared for a possible attack, fortifying twelve farmhouses into garrisons. They did not, however, expect the ferocity with which "a body of two hundred and fifty Indians, collected from the tribes of St. John, Penobscot and Norridgewog, attended by a French priest," attacked the morning of July 18. Five of the garrisons fell, as well as dozens of other homes. At Adams's garrison, fourteen died, including a woman whose womb was ripped open and the fetus destroyed. The attackers arrived at Beard's garrison, on Beard's Creek, which combines with Littlehole Creek to form a marshy inlet north of Oyster River, too late, as the inhabitants had escaped to the river. Belknap told of the "singular manner" by which Thomas Bickford defended his garrisoned home alone: "He kept up a constant fire at them, changing his dress as often as he could, shewing himself with a different cap, hat or coat, and sometimes without either, and giving directions aloud as if he had a number of men with him."

The last garrison attacked was Woodman's, which was preserved from destruction and survived into the twentieth century before being destroyed by fire. Woodman's was situated between Beard's and Littlehole Creeks. John Woodman had arrived at Oyster River in 1657, had been granted acreage, was a captain of the militia and represented Dover at the General Court. The house was built similarly to other garrisons of the time and place, a saltbox built on a sturdy stone foundation with a central chimney, thick walls, plentiful windows and an upstairs supported by large, thick wooden beams. The door was strong, and the house was surrounded by a wooden palisade of sorts that might slow down rather than stop attackers. The people in the Woodman garrison escaped destruction, but the owners of twenty houses as well as ninety-four people did not. Other Piscataqua locations were similarly attacked, including the outskirts of Portsmouth, where raiders descended upon the Cutt farm, killing the matron of the house, Ursula Cutt, widow of the former president of New Hampshire John Cutt.

Such attacks were sporadic and, to the defenders, apparently random, the motives of the attackers difficult to understand, the reasons for such suffering unclear. In June 1696, raiders canoed from York on the Maine coast to the Piscataqua, where they raided several farms at Portsmouth plain, killing fourteen and kidnapping four. Pursued, the Indians fled south to Breakfast Hill (in Rye), where the militia freed the prisoners but could not engage the attackers. The raiders fled through a swamp, recovered their canoes and had the wherewithal to canoe offshore to the Isles of Shoals under cover of darkness, round the islands on the east side and proceed north up the coast. Part of the motive for these attacks was revenge for the duplicitous behavior of Major Waldron and the Piscataqua militia in 1676. Major Charles Frost, a leading inhabitant of Kittery and participant in Waldron's trick on the Indians, became the focus on their revenge in 1697, when in July he was assassinated. Shortly thereafter the Peace of Ryswick, ending the European war, led to the cessation of hostilities and peace, if temporary, in northern New England. The number of Piscataqua residents killed in King William's War totaled 280, the number kidnapped, 96.

QUEEN ANNE'S WAR AND DUMMER'S WAR

The pretensions and jealousies of the kings and queens of Europe could hardly guarantee a long-lasting peace, and war again erupted between the French and English in 1703. Queen Anne's War lasted for a decade and featured the same sporadic attacks as before on the inhabitants of the Piscataqua Valley. Garrisoned houses became the center of community life; boys aspiring to be men took charge of family affairs while fathers marched in militia bands in pursuit of the enemy; women became adept at loading muskets and bandaging wounds; and farms and fields lay neglected under the curse of the apprehension of sudden attack. Indian raiders traveled in small bands, eluding discovery, attacking individuals or small groups who could not mount a defense. Here and there, month by month, one or two were killed or captured at Lamprey River, Oyster River, Dover and Exeter, but the numbers of the dead could not match the much greater number of inhabitants who lived in continual fear. The inhabitants of Maine, New Hampshire and Massachusetts, having learned from the experiences of King William's War, were better prepared for defense and retaliation in Queen Anne's War, and there were fewer casualties. The old fortification on Great Island, called the Castle, was strengthened first during King William's War and, during Queen Anne's War in 1705, stone walls were put in place. "The frontiers were well guarded," Belknap wrote:

> One half of the militia did duty at the garrisons and were ready to march at a minute's warning; a scout of forty men kept ranging on the heads of the towns, and the like care

was taken by sea, spy-boats being employed in coasting from Cape Neddock [York, Maine] *to the Great Boar's head* [on the New Hampshire coast at Hampton].

Eventually the Peace of Utrecht put an end to apprehension and military preparedness, for the time being.

With the accession of King George I in 1715, a new governor was appointed for New Hampshire and Massachusetts—Colonel Samuel Shute, who relied on his lieutenant governors, notably John Wentworth, to perform the daily activities of administering the two colonies. Having been a counselor under Shute's predecessor Joseph Dudley, Wentworth was a native of New Hampshire, grandson of William Wentworth, an original settler of Exeter and longtime resident of Dover, and a successful merchant. He served as lieutenant governor for thirteen years until his death in 1730. For a time under Wentworth, the Piscataqua Valley was free from war, which allowed for a focus on more peaceful activities, in particular making a living from the fruits of the forest. Settlers on the Newichawannock, Cocheco, Oyster, Lamprey and Squamscot Rivers cultivated the soil for food, chiefly maize, and harvested the forests for timber, masts and naval stores. A bone of contention between the inhabitants and the government was the British policy of reserving white pine trees that were two feet in diameter for use as masts in the British navy. Government surveyors ranged the woods, even on private land, marking likely trees with the "broad arrow." The inhabitants typically knew how to get around the law, but were still disgusted at its presumption upon their rights of personal property. Inhabitants who had pitch pine forests used these trees for tar and turpentine. Others cultivated hemp for use as rope. Still others harvested iron ore and built ironworks, where they used large charcoal fires to smelt the iron ore, forming it into usable bar iron. A favored location for this activity was the Lamprey River. Growth meant the creation of new towns, such as Greenland, which separated from Portsmouth in 1705; Newington, which separated from Dover in 1713; Berwick, which separated from Kittery in 1713; and Stratham, which separated from Exeter in 1716. Stratham, named for an English baron, friend to Governor Shute, was originally part of the Squamscot Patent, situated across the Squamscot River from Exeter, forming the southern shore of Great Bay.

Meanwhile difficult relations continued between the French and their Indian allies and the English. At issue in 1721 was the religious differences between the English and the French, which would eventually lead to the three-year conflict known as Dummer's War. The New England colonies had been founded at a time of religious warfare in Europe involving years of bloodshed between Protestants of northern Europe and Catholics of southern Europe. During the late 1600s and early 1700s, the religious differences between the Puritan and Anglican British Americans of New England and the Catholics of New France added venom to the political conflict over the control of North America. The Abenaki, like other American Indian tribes, were more apt to listen to the French missionaries who lived among them and taught them the ways of Catholicism. Those Indians who converted to Christianity usually became Catholics rather than Protestants because, in the words of one Indian chief, "the French have taught us to pray to God, which the English never did." The French encouraged their religious protégés to make religious war upon the British American settlements, particularly the outlying ones of upstate New York, eastern Maine and the Piscataqua Valley, which were easiest to attack.

In 1722 Sebastian Ralle (Sebastien Rale), a Jesuit who had lived among the Indians of the Kennebec Valley at the village of Norridgewog for decades, mentoring them and ministering to their needs, incited them to free the hunting lands of the Penobscot and Kennebec Rivers from English impositions. New Hampshire and Massachusetts militia commanders determined that Ralle's religious influence over the Abenakis had to end, so attempted to capture him. They failed to abduct Ralle, though succeeded in infuriating the Indians to begin their attacks upon colonial settlements once again. Militias were again organized and troops sent on patrol. As an incentive for the soldiers, the provincial government proclaimed that every Indian scalp returned to Boston would be redeemed for one hundred pounds. Even so, Indian raiders made sporadic attacks upon Piscataqua settlements, first at Dover, then Lamprey River, then Oyster River. Overall few inhabitants were killed and the colonials successfully brought the war to the Indians, attacking the Abenaki settlement at Norridgewog (and killing Father Ralle) and winning a Pyrrhic victory at the battle of Lovewell's Pond in Fryeburg. Terms of peace were decided upon between British and French provincial authorities at the end of 1725, thus ending Dummer's War.

EXPANDING SETTLEMENTS

One consequence of the war was that an initial path for a road was laid out from Cocheco Falls to Lake Winnipesaukee, upon which settlers journeyed up the Cocheco, founding in 1728 the town of Rochester. As the Piscataqua Valley grew in population, and the enterprising sought to settle the lands of the inland tributaries of the Piscataqua, to be inhabited by the young and adventurous, land speculators with wealth and connections to those with influence at the court of King George applied to the king to be granted charters for new townships. The king in turn granted charters to proprietors with the stipulation that they or their surrogates found the township and settle the land within a certain time period. The charter for the township of Rochester, for example, dated May 1722, stipulates "that the Proprietors of every share…build a dwelling house within three years and settle a family therein and break up three Acres of Ground and Plant or sow the same within four years…That a Meeting house be built for the Publick worship of God within the s'd term of four years." The king further required that "all Mast trees growing on the s'd Tract of land" be reserved for his use. The king granted

unto the s'd Grantees to appoint and hold Town and Proprietors Meetings from time to time as occasion requires and to chuse all officers that are proper for the management of Town and Proprietary affairs with all the powers privileges & authoritys which any other Town within this Province hath enjoy'd doth enjoy or ought to enjoy according to the laws customs & usages thereof.

Churchgoers at Newcastle, originally called Great Island, separated from Portsmouth to create First Parish in the late 1600s. *Courtesy of Benjamin Lawson.*

The practice of granting to proprietors the rights and privileges to settle towns and reap the initial fruits of their planting was in accord with the founding of New Hampshire, originally granted to royal favorites as a means to build their personal fortunes. Proprietors of Rochester, for example, included Governor Shute, Lieutenant Governor John Wentworth and councilmembers such as Richard Waldron. The towns of Nottingham and Barrington were chartered at the same time as Rochester; Barrington was settled a short time later, in 1732, built on the Isinglass River, which flows into the Cocheco. Nottingham was initially settled in 1727, but mostly remained a frontier outpost, a place for hunters and traders until the 1760s.

Expansion of Piscataqua settlements and growing population brought other growing pains besides warfare. Notable was the throat distemper that swept through New England from 1735 to 1736. The Piscataqua Valley was hit hard. Hundreds of children died: in Exeter, 105; in Kittery, 122; in Portsmouth, 99. Dover lost 77 children. Newington (known as Bloody Point until formed as a new parish in 1714, when the name changed) lost 16. Even new settlements such as Newmarket, an independent parish that separated from Exeter in 1727, lost 20 children. Chester, near the source of the Squamscot, saw 21 children die. Oyster River, incorporated as Durham in 1732, lost 79. Hints of the suffering and despair that the epidemic brought to the Piscataqua Valley can still be seen in local cemeteries, where gravestones of dead children tell a laconic, somber tale. At the graveyard at School House Hill in Durham there are several such stones. One is for Mary Stephenson, which is decorated by acanthus leaves. Nearby is another stone, nameless save for the initials B.S., a child of fourteen who died of the distemper in 1735. The stone for eleven-year-old M.W. stands close by. Some families lost two, three or more children to the disease in the space of days. The distemper baffled physicians, who, practicing medicine before the onset of germ theory in the 1800s, declared that it was spread from "some occult quality in the air." "The general description" of the disease, Belknap wrote, "was a swelled throat, with white or ash-colored specks, an efflorescence on the skin, great debility of the whole system, and a strong tendency to putridity." The symptoms resembled scarlet fever and diphtheria, both of which were horrible childhood diseases before the age of antibiotics reduced their occurrence and severity.

Such domestic disasters encouraged greater consternation about the hereafter in both the dying and living. At this time of the 1730s and 1740s, in New England there was a widespread religious revival known as the Great Awakening. The revival left few parishes free from controversy between those who embraced the revival—the New Lights—and the Old Lights, who favored a steadier traditional approach to Christianity. An example of the former was Nicholas Gilman, a native of Exeter who served several parishes, in Kingston, Newmarket and Portsmouth, before becoming pastor of the First Parish in Durham. There he fully embraced the Awakening, which involved a highly emotional Christianity, wherein believers would openly weep and cry out because of their sins and helplessness before the wrath of God. Gilman encouraged such antics in his parishioners, who were nicknamed the "Durham Dancers." Gilman wore himself out at an early age, dying in 1748. He was buried in Exeter. The most well-known Old

Light minister—though he preached at Portsmouth for a brief time and much later than Gilman—was Ezra Stiles, a graduate of Yale, who served the North Parish from 1777 to 1778, leaving to become president of Yale College.

The governor of both New Hampshire and Massachusetts at this time was Jonathan Belcher, who had assumed office in 1730. Belcher, a Massachusetts native, was sophisticated, wealthy, vain and candid. His lieutenant governor, Colonel David Dunbar, was just as proud as Belcher and intent on undermining the governor's authority. Internal political struggles highlighted New Hampshire politics in the 1730s—not until 1744 would a common enemy arise, the French and Indians, to unite the province and its leaders in a purpose larger than private political gain. Belcher usually stayed in Boston and rarely traveled to New Hampshire; Dunbar was more often at the Piscataqua in his office as surveyor of the king's woods. Dunbar, used to command, was heavy-handed in his enforcement of the provision that suitable white pines must be left untouched, even on private land, awaiting the will of the king. The only exception was an exemption granted by the government permitting the use of trees. The hardy farmers and lumberjacks of the upper Piscataqua thought such licenses were nonsense and believed that trees on private property were to be used by the owner. Belknap, who lived among such men and women, wrote,

> Dunbar went to the saw mills; where he seized and marked large quantities of lumber; and with an air and manner to which he had been accustomed in his military capacity, abused and threatened the people. That class of men, with whom he was disposed to contend, are not easily intimidated with high words; and he was not a match for them, in that species of controversy, which they have denominated swamp law.

On two separate occasions in 1734, Dunbar butted heads with the people of the Cocheco and Squamscot, and came out the loser. At Dover, Dunbar tried to seize logs at a mill operated by Paul Gerrish, who when threatened with death from the king's surveyor, responded in kind with such force that Dunbar relented and departed. At Brentwood, then part of Exeter, the inhabitants (in the guise of Indians) beat the surveyor's men and sabotaged their boat, in what came to be known as the Mast Tree Riot. Such domestic quarrels, however, paled in comparison to the much greater quarrel with the French, which would soon erupt in the form of King George's War.

THE WENTWORTH ADMINISTRATION

When war once again came to the Piscataqua Valley, New Hampshire and Massachusetts had been separated into two separate provinces, the former governed by Benning Wentworth, the latter by William Shirley. Wentworth was a Portsmouth merchant and son of former Lieutenant Governor John Wentworth. He received the gubernatorial appointment because of his financial problems and connections with the English aristocracy, specifically the duke of Newcastle. Throughout Wentworth's administration, from 1741 to 1767, the governor used his office to enrich himself by appointing himself the king's surveyor and by granting lands to proprietors, including himself. During Wentworth's administration, the Piscataqua Valley suffered through two wars, King George's War (1744–49), and the French and Indian War (1755–63).

King George's War began as most imperial wars did, as a dispute between rival empires. In this case, France and England wrangled over control of Nova Scotia, which had been granted to the British in the Treaty of Utrecht in 1713. The French had retained control of Cape Breton, an island off the coast of Nova Scotia. During the years since Queen Anne's War, the French built a strong fortress called Louisburg on the southeast corner of Cape Breton. This fortress, in Belknap's words,

> *was, in peace, a safe retreat for the ships of France bound homeward from the East and West-Indies; and in war, a source of distress to the northern English colonies; its situation being extremely favorable for privateers to ruin their fishery and interrupt their coasting and foreign trade; for which reasons, the reduction of it was an object as desirable to them, as that of Carthage was to the Romans.*

When word arrived in 1744 of the outbreak of hostilities in Europe, the French of Cape Breton immediately invaded and took possession of the English fishing port of Canso (Canseau), an island off the coast of Nova Scotia that was a center of English fishing operations. The English responded with a daring attack on Louisburg under the command of William Pepperrell Jr. of Kittery. The elder William Pepperrell had immigrated to America in the mid-1600s, and after a time living at the Isles of Shoals moved to Kittery, where he married the daughter of a leading merchant, John Bray, and established himself as a merchant, landowner and local leader. William and Margery Pepperrell had a son, William, in 1693. The younger Pepperrell was raised with aristocratic sensibilities, learning the arts of war, sailing, landowning and trade. By the early 1700s, the Pepperrells exported lumber and fish to various ports in the French and British empires, particularly the West Indies, and imported products such as sugar and molasses. Their fleet of ships included brigantines, schooners and sloops. They bought land in Kittery and north toward Casco Bay; William Pepperrell Jr. owned most of Kittery Point, including the fortification that became in time Fort McClary. Like the elder Pepperrell, the younger was active in politics, serving as a local representative to the Massachusetts General Court, a chief justice and an officer in the militia, rising to colonel, in charge of defending the Maine coast. He became intimate with the Boston merchant and political elite, married Mary Hirst and was close to Massachusetts Governor Jonathan Belcher. In the 1740s, Pepperrell's military experience and wealth recommended him to Governor William Shirley, who with Pepperrell and Portsmouth resident William Vaughan conceived of the bold plan to march upon Louisburg. Pepperrell raised three thousand troops from Massachusetts and New Hampshire, which sailed north to Canso, then laid siege to Louisburg, which lasted until June, when the French capitulated. Pepperrell's success in leading untrained colonials to take a French stronghold endeared him to colonials and the English alike.

Benning Wentworth, governor of New Hampshire from 1741 to 1767, lived at this rambling mansion next to the Piscataqua River in Portsmouth. This print dates from the early twentieth century. *From* Vignettes of Portsmouth.

Fort McClary had three levels: this photograph is of the lower level. *Courtesy of Benjamin Lawson.*

King George II made Pepperrell a baron, and he was promoted to be the highest-ranking American officer in the British army. The only sour note in Sir William's rise to fame was the Treaty of Aix-la-Chapelle (1748), which ended King George's War and returned Louisburg to the French.

Before the treaty and after the success at Louisburg, during the years from 1745 to 1748, Piscataqua Valley residents again suffered the bane of warfare. To prepare for what appeared to be certain French attacks on the coast, the colonists strengthened the defenses of Fort William and Mary at Newcastle and also fortified Odiorne's Point. The fortification on Pepperrell land, at this time called Fort William, guarded the northern entrance to the river. Colonel Theodore Atkinson, who was a native of Newcastle and a resident of Portsmouth, a longtime secretary of the province and member of the council, was made commander of the militia, and towns mustered men for action. However, most of the military action during King George's War occurred along the Connecticut River Valley. Indian attacks on the Piscataqua Valley were rare and limited to the upper tributaries. Warriors repeatedly attacked Rochester, for example, killing isolated people.

Fort McClary from across Piscataqua. The walls and blockhouse of Fort McClary, from the perspective of Fort Constitution across the water, rise above the northern shore of the Piscataqua. *Courtesy of Benjamin Lawson.*

These seemingly impregnable walls of Fort Constitution were constructed early in the 1800s. *Courtesy of Benjamin Lawson.*

The Treaty of Aix-la-Chapelle of 1748 brought peace to the Piscataqua, if only for a time, as the causes of conflict between the French and English remained unresolved, and would again spill over into war in 1755—the French and Indian War. The action in this war centered on the Connecticut River, down which French and Indian attackers went to attack Fort Number Four and other bastions of colonial defense. Piscataqua soldiers were involved only insofar that they joined in the defense of New Hampshire or went on the offense against the enemy, joining corps of rangers such as that led by Major Robert Rogers. In this final conflict between the French and English for control of North America, the English were victorious. In the Treaty of Paris of 1763, the French gave up their lands in North America to the English. Belknap wrote,

The conquest of Canada gave peace to the frontiers of New-Hampshire, after a turbulent scene of fifteen years; in which, with very little intermission, they had been

distressed by the enemy. Many captives returned to their homes; and friends who had long been separated, embraced each other in peace. The joy was heightened by this consideration, that the country of Canada, being subdued, could no longer be a source of terror and distress.

CHAPTER FOUR

THE PISCATAQUA DURING THE REVOLUTION

During the events leading to and occurring during the American War for Independence (1763–83), the Piscataqua Valley played an important role in the maritime conflict with England. Whereas the center of action in previous wars occurred on the frontiers of the tributaries of the Piscataqua, the towns with the biggest role during the American Revolution were the centers of trade and shipbuilding, such as Portsmouth, Kittery and Exeter. Whereas in some American communities the opposition to British policies centered on issues of sovereignty, taxes and restrictions on movement, Piscataqua Patriots opposed the British because of unfair trade laws and practices. After the outbreak of the war in 1775, the Piscataqua contributed up to one hundred privateers to fight the British navy, built warships such as the *Providence* and *Raleigh*, waged war along the northern New England coast, furnished militia troops to fight in such engagements as the battle of Bennington and provided military and political leadership in the persons of John Sullivan and John Langdon.

The end of one war, the French and Indian War, initiated a new war, the precursory events of which began in 1763, as soon as the Treaty of Paris was signed. The British found themselves in control of the lands once occupied by the French, including the Ohio and Mississippi Valleys, the Great Lakes, the St. Lawrence River, Quebec and Nova Scotia. The British empire in North America quadrupled and now included a volatile mixture of French Catholics, English Protestants and Indians who had only known the English as inveterate enemies. British leaders of Parliament and King George III determined that new policies must be put into effect to administer their expanded empire efficiently. Acts for regulating the export trade of the colonies had been on the books for a century, though they were rarely enforced. The king decided to enforce these laws and established admiralty courts to try cases of illegal trade. Added to this was a tariff placed on items of trade such as molasses, a major New England import. The colonies had always conceded the right of the British to regulate trade, so that these new measures caused little beyond grumbling.

The Liberty Pole was originally erected by Portsmouth Sons of Liberty in opposition to the 1765 Stamp Act; the present pole dates from 1824. *Courtesy of Benjamin Lawson.*

The Stamp Act of 1765 was, however, a different matter. This act required a tax in the form of a stamp to be paid for all legal and commercial documents. The tax was only a few pence, but the colonials were outraged that the British should presume to enact a stamp on local and provincial domestic and personal affairs. The reaction of the populace was swift. In Portsmouth, as in other cities, bands of men organized themselves into troops that marched through the streets to the beat of a drum. These Sons of Liberty declared themselves opponents of supposed British attempts to impose controls on local and provincial affairs where they had never before had power. The Piscataqua stamp agent, George Meserve—son of one of the heroes of the French and Indian War, Nathaniel Meserve—arrived by ship at Boston Harbor with the stamps in September 9, 1765. The Boston Sons of Liberty, however, threatened to sink the boat and its nefarious stamps. Meserve relented and wrote a letter promising not to issue the stamps. By September 11, however, word came that the Portsmouth Sons of Liberty were trying Meserve in a court of admiralty. An effigy of Meserve served as replacement for the stamp agent himself. Meserve (or rather, his effigy) was found guilty and sentenced to hang by the neck next to the devil. This done, the next day Merserve's effigy and company were burned. Merserve's effigy was tried and hung in Dover as well. The day the Stamp Act was to take effect, November 1, 1765, the Sons of Liberty of Portsmouth orchestrated a theatrical response: "The bells tolled," wrote Belknap, "and a funeral procession was made for the Goddess of Liberty; but on depositing her in the grave, some signs of life were supposed to discovered, and she was carried off in triumph. By such exhibitions, the spirit of the populace was kept up; though the minds of the most thoughtful persons were filled with anxiety." Such popular demonstrations—even violence in some colonies—against the stamps convinced the British that they had misjudged the colonials. The Stamp Act was repealed, though replaced by the Declaratory Act, in which Parliament declared its sovereignty over the colonies in all respects. For the time being, however, the repeal of the Stamp Act brought joy to Piscataqua Sons of Liberty, who in May, in Portsmouth, Exeter and Dover, put on dinners, parades, fireworks and other entertainment in celebration of its repeal.

CONFLICT COMES TO THE PISCATAQUA

Meanwhile, Governor Benning Wentworth was coming under attack for some of his practices, including nepotism in the appointment of colonial officials and irregularities in land grants to favorites (and himself). He was forced to resign in 1767, his successor being his nephew, John Wentworth. The new governor was a wealthy merchant who had acted as agent for New Hampshire in London and who had friends at the royal court. He had advocated repeal of the Stamp Act but for economic rather than political reasons. He was moderate and generally popular with the people of the Piscataqua and did his best to preserve the peace at a time when the forces of revolution were working against it.

This anchor, on the grounds of the Wentworth-Coolidge Mansion, recalls days long past when great mast ships anchored at Portsmouth harbor. *Courtesy of Benjamin Lawson.*

Wentworth's patience was tested on several occasions, the first time in October 1771, when Collector of Customs George Meserve impounded a Piscataqua vessel for smuggling molasses, evading the nine pence duty on each gallon. Portsmouth Patriots responded by sneaking aboard the ship, confining the customs officials on guard, then unloading and hiding the molasses. In 1773 Piscataqua Patriots joined the opposition up and down the American coast against the British Tea Act, which imposed a modest duty on tea imports in America. The reaction by Americans was both violent, as in Boston, where the Boston Tea Party occurred, and peaceful, as in Portsmouth, where the people demanded that tea shipments be halted and redirected to other parts of the empire, such as Nova Scotia. Wentworth, as the representative of the king in New Hampshire, became the object of scorn for Piscataqua Patriots. Some residents of the Piscataqua, such as Jeremy Belknap, were uncertain whether such vehement opposition to the British government and its executive was best. Belknap, who admired Wentworth and believed that assaults on his character were unjust, swore a "Deposition in Favor of Governor Wentworth" on January 4, 1773:

> *I, Jeremy Belknap, minister of the Gospel, in Dover, in his Majesty's Province of New Hampshire, testify & declare—That I have lived in this Province about eight years, and that since John Wentworth, Esq., was appointed to the chief seat of government therein, so far as I have had opportunity to hear & observe, he hath merited the esteem of the people in general among whom I have lived & conversed, & hath in divers instances*

shewn a just regard to the true interest of the Province, in connexion with his Majesty's service; particularly in encouraging learning and agriculture, by reason of which the Province is much advanced in value & reputation. And I do not know that the people suffer any injuries or grievances of which the said Governor ought to bear the blame. And so far as I am capable of judging, I believe that, if a general suffrage were called for, it would be in favour of his continuance in office.

The Boston Port Bill of 1774, which was the British response to the Boston Tea Party, closed Boston Harbor and imposed martial law in Massachusetts. In turn, the response to these "Intolerable Acts" in New Hampshire, as well as in other colonies, was fear and apprehension along with action. When a general congress of representatives of the thirteen colonies was proposed to meet in Philadelphia, New Hampshire Revolutionary leaders met at Exeter and selected two delegates. Because the governor and council sat at Portsmouth, Exeter assumed a role as the locus of Revolutionary activities. Two militia leaders, Nathaniel Folsom and John Sullivan of Durham, were sent to Philadelphia as New Hampshire's delegates. In this state of affairs of opposition to an established government, Revolutionary committees were formed in all of the thirteen colonies. Piscataqua men formed a "committee of safety" that agreed on the Portsmouth Tea Resolves, which strongly encouraged Piscataqua merchants not to import and sell British tea. Piscataqua Revolutionaries also took one of the first military actions of the coming war.

Governor Wentworth was friends with Jeremy Belknap; the two men shared an interest in human and natural history, and Wentworth assisted the historian in acquiring documents relating to New Hampshire's past. Belknap sent manuscript chapters of his book for the governor's critical comments. In a letter from Wentworth to Belknap in November 1774, Wentworth sent Belknap an account of the journey of Nicholas Austin to the White Mountains and ascent of the highest, Mount Washington, in October 1774. Austin was a firm Loyalist who had recruited workers in Piscataqua towns to journey to Boston to help General Thomas Gage fortify the city, recently taken over by British troops as a consequence of the Coercive Acts. Wentworth was friends with Austin, and decried that "some modern patriots at Rochester tyrannically insulted and abused [him] for the sake of Liberty." Wentworth fooled himself into thinking that such actions were going to lessen rather than worsen.

I wou'd not infest you with a syllable on politics [the governor wrote], *but that I am convinc'd it will give satisfaction to your benevolent heart to hear that it is probable, at least it is in my opinion, the clouds of distraction begin to disperse, and that there is some prospect of a civil creation soon emerging out of the present chaotic jumble of discordant political elements. That it may speedily rest upon its center and assume the fair form of Peace, Charity, universal safety, and wisest subordination, must be the anxious desire of all that cordially wish prosperity to America, in which number is surely included, as I verily beleive* [sic], *both yourself and your sincere friend, J. Wentworth*

Less than a month after this letter, the Piscataqua Committee of Safety gained intelligence that the British were to send a naval frigate and soldiers to reinforce Fort William and Mary on Great Island. Revolutionaries led by John Sullivan and John Langdon descended upon the fort in mid-December, imprisoned the small garrison and carried away powder, arms and cannons. Governor Wentworth's response was to declare these men outlaws and demand that all citizens of New Hampshire assist in their apprehension. Instead, the leaders of the attack, Sullivan and Langdon, were elected representatives of the Second Continental Congress, which met in 1775 in Philadelphia. Governor Wentworth, to his credit, worked tirelessly to bring about a reconciliation of people and king in New Hampshire, but outside events nullified his efforts.

THE ONSET OF WAR

On April 19, 1775, in response to information that Massachusetts Patriots had stores of musket balls and black powder at Concord, west of Boston, General Gage ordered British Regular troops—the redcoats—to confiscate the material and arrest rebels. The troops marched through Lexington, where they had a brief bloody confrontation with the town militia, then Concord, where a longer battle raged. Frustrated in their efforts, the British retreated, but by the time they marched back to Boston, militia from Massachusetts and neighboring states including New Hampshire, had lined the road waiting to fire upon the redcoats. Men from the Piscataqua Valley participated in the battle. Jeremy Belknap happened to be at Knight's Ferry between Dover Point and Bloody Point when he heard the news. His parents, Joseph and Mary Byles Belknap, and sister Abigail lived on Milk Street in Boston. Belknap knew he had to go help them depart the beleaguered city and come to Dover to live. Belknap penned a hasty note to his wife Ruth (quoted in Jane Belknap Marcou, *Life of Jeremy Belknap*):

> *My Dear*
> *Before you receive this you will hear the awful news by the Express I met just now at the ferry, of the devastation the troops have made at Concord, and the commencement of a civil war, which makes it absolutely necessary that I should proceed immediately to Boston (if it is not in ashes before I get there). I shall try to get a chaise at Greenland. As necessity has no laws, the people must excuse my absence next Sabbath, if I should not return before it. Your affectionate husband,*
> *J.B.*
> *N.B. The Dragoons have arrived at Boston.*

The pastor was ultimately successful, and his father, mother and sister came to Dover to live out the remainder of their lives.

The inauguration of war changed the lives of other Piscataqua families. Governor John Wentworth realized that war meant his position as governor was untenable. In the summer of 1775, he abandoned his post and with his family sought safe haven on the

British frigate *Scarborough*, riding at anchor in Portsmouth harbor. He left the province, never to return, in July.

Piscataqua Patriots quickly took charge in the power vacuum made final by Wentworth's departure. The provincial congress, meeting at Exeter, which had negated Wentworth's authority after the war began in April, continued to meet during the summer and into autumn. Assuming temporary legislative and executive authority, the congress appointed a committee of safety to carry out day-to-day executive power, ordered the building and reinforcing of fortifications to protect the harbor, instituted a full ban on importation of British goods and organized the militia and commissioned officers. Every town already had militia that had trained on town greens and had learned how to march and to obey orders. All men owned at least a musket, and with few exceptions were required to muster if they were able-bodied and under sixty years of age. Towns kept powder, balls and flint. Committees of inspection and correspondence increasingly took control of town affairs, organizing town defenses, enlisting men to fight and intimidating those who remained loyal to the king. The provincial congress raised three regiments, commanded by John Stark, James Reed and Enoch Poor of Exeter. The Continental Congress, meanwhile, appointed John Sullivan a brigadier general. In October 1775, after the British had destroyed Falmouth, Maine, and Piscataqua residents were apprehensive that the same might happen to Portsmouth, Commander-in-Chief George Washington ordered General Sullivan to the Piscataqua to take charge of its defense. Already two forts had been constructed on two islands in the Piscataqua—Fort Washington on Peirce Island and Fort Sullivan on Seavey's Island. Sullivan reinforced these two forts as well as the Castle (previously called Fort William and Mary), and the fortifications on Kittery Point (Fort William), which had once belonged to the Pepperrells, but they had stayed loyal to the king. Kittery confiscated their lands, and Sullivan now fortified the point.

John Sullivan was the oldest son of John Sullivan Sr., an Irish immigrant who was a schoolteacher in Berwick, and elder brother of the Maine historian and statesman James Sullivan. The older brother relocated a few miles west to Durham, where he opened a law practice and bought a graceful estate on the shores of the Oyster River at the head of tide. John Adams rode the circuit courts in Maine at the same time as James Sullivan, met his brother John and described John Sullivan's Oyster River estate in a 1774 letter to his wife, Abigail:

> *I find that the country is the situation to make estates by the law. John Sullivan, who is placed at Durham, in New Hampshire, is younger, both in years and practice, than I am. He began with nothing, but is now said to be worth ten thousand pounds, lawful money…He has a fine stream of water, with an excellent corn-mill, saw-mill, fulling-mill, scythe-mill and others, in all, six mills, which are both his delight and his profit. As he has earned cash in his business at the bar, he has taken opportunities to purchase farms of his neighbors, who wanted to sell and move out further into the woods, at an advantageous rate, and in this way has been growing rich. Under the smiles and auspices of Governor Wentworth, he has been promoted in the civil and military way, so that he is treated with great respect in this neighborhood.*

Governor Wentworth appointed John Sullivan a major in the provincial militia in 1772. Sullivan, far from recompensing the governor, headed the resistance against him in New Hampshire, serving as a delegate in the First and Second Continental Congresses and joining the raid on Fort William and Mary in 1774. When the war broke out in 1775, he was made a brigadier general of the Continental army; a year later Congress appointed him major general. During his five-year service in the Continental army, Sullivan commanded troops in Massachusetts, New York, Rhode Island, Pennsylvania and New Hampshire. His reputation was sufficiently solid upon his retirement from the Continental troops in 1780 that he served in various capacities for the state, including representative to Congress, commander of the militia and attorney general. He was a district judge, president of New Hampshire and a delegate at the Constitutional Convention that ratified the U.S. Constitution in 1788.

Many years before, when the state of New Hampshire began in November 1775, elections were held to establish an independent state government. Each town selected representatives to meet at a central location, at this time Exeter, to meet as a state legislature. Only property owners could hold office; indeed, there was a modest property qualification for the suffrage as well. The state legislature voted on a bicameral legislature, the second house being a council charged with executive authority. The president of the council was the president of the state—the first president was Meshech Weare of Hampton, who served throughout the war. Weare, wrote Belknap,

> *was not a person of original inventive genius, but had a clear discernment, extensive knowledge, accurate judgment, calm temper, a modest deportment, an upright and benevolent heart, and a habit of prudence and diligence in discharging the various duties of public and private life. He did not enrich himself by his public employment, but was one of those good men, "who dare to love their country and be poor."*

The war brought conflicting feelings to many inhabitants, who heretofore believed themselves subjects of Great Britain loyal to King George III. This was certainly the case with Jeremy Belknap, who did not want war, was a reluctant Patriot—as so many at the time were—and hoped and prayed for reconciliation and peace. Even as late as June 26, 1776, when the Declaration of Independence was being drafted in Philadelphia, Belknap's sermons were conciliatory toward the British government, hoping that war could still be averted, yet knowing that God alone would decide.

THE WAR AT SEA

Besides contributing soldiers and officers to the American land forces, Piscataqua towns also supported American naval operations, particularly by building warships and by outfitting privateers to prey on British shipping. Before the war, Piscataqua overseas trade focused on the British Empire, particularly islands of the Caribbean such as Barbados, Granada, Jamaica and Antigua. Not only was this trade halted by the Revolution, but

The Piscataqua During the Revolution

British warships also patrolled coastal waters, including the mouth of the Piscataqua, to prevent American vessels from engaging in trade and fishing. Privation hit Portsmouth, Kittery and the other mercantile, fishing and shipbuilding centers of the Piscataqua Valley. New Hampshire, like other former colonies, suffered from rising prices brought about by demand for goods outpacing supply. There was little gold or silver specie available in the new United States, so that individual states issued paper money based on questionable financial resources. The town records of Portsmouth, for example, provide evidence of the suffering of the poor during the war years. Town officials petitioned the state legislature in 1776 that the "Poor on the Isles of Shoals be relieved out of the Public Treasury, to ease the Burthens of this Town which has been at great Expense on their Account, & at a time when we are unable to Maintain our own." By 1779 the cost of maintaining the poor rose to an astounding (albeit inflationary) £30,000. Within a year the cost rose to £80,000!

"Multitudes are reduced from easy Circumstances," the town records lamented, "to want & beggary, and half the Inhabitants at least have frequently been without Bread or Fuel." The town records further reported that shipping tonnage had declined from 12,000 tons in 1774 to 500 tons in 1780—as a result the "Mechanic & Labourer" were unemployed and in want. The disabled, particularly soldiers and widows, suffered the most. Although Portsmouth already had a workhouse to work the poor and a house of correction to punish the idle beggar, the town continued to spend sums for the relief of the deserving poor. For instance, the town spent £2,905 on eight families of soldiers in 1781.

The most thriving segment of the Piscataqua economy during the war was privateering, the outfitting with small cannon of a private vessel to engage in state-sponsored piracy. With a practically nonexistent U.S. Navy at the beginning of the war, the Continental Congress authorized states to grant letters of marque to private shipowners to recruit sailors to capture enemy ships and tow the prizes to port. There, an admiralty judge would divide up the prize between crew, owner and investors. Scores of Portsmouth vessels engaged in privateering during the war. Leading Piscataqua merchants owned or invested in the sloops, brigs and ships of between two and twenty guns. John Taylor Gilman of Exeter, who would become the governor of New Hampshire, invested in the *Adventure*. Exeter shipbuilder James Hackett also invested in privateers. Eliphalet Ladd of Exeter built the *Hercules*, a twenty-gun privateer that was quickly captured by the British. Dr. Joshua Brackett, a Portsmouth physician, owned shares in the privateer *John Bunyan*; he was also, surprisingly, the judge of the admiralty court in Portsmouth that determined the legitimacy and value of captured prizes brought to port by privateers. Demand for sailors was great, and ship captains advertised in the local *New Hampshire Gazette*. The following advertisement appeared in the summer of 1781:

> *My Jolly Tars take Notice—*
> *That the remarkably fast-sailing Privateer Cutter Greyhound, is now compleatly fixed for, and next Wednesday will sail on a Ten Weeks Cruize. Those hearty Lads who are desirous of embracing the Golden Opportunity of making their own Fortunes, must immediately apply at the Rendezvous at Mrs. Shortridge's on Spring Hill, where they shall receive every Encouragement that a generous Soul can wish.*

The *Greyhound* had success lying off the coast of Nova Scotia preying on British fishing shallops.

One of the biggest investors in Piscataqua privateers was John Langdon, who had his hand in boats such as the *Alexander, Hector, Portsmouth, Amphitrite, Bennington, Swan, Fair American, Blossom, Hazard* and *Fox*. Langdon, as a Portsmouth representative to the Continental Congress, was charged with building vessels for the burgeoning U.S. Navy. Langdon oversaw the building of the *Raleigh* in 1776. Langdon was a wealthy merchant and former ship captain who was one of the first among the conservative Portsmouth merchants to embrace wholeheartedly the idea of independence from England. The *Raleigh* was to be one of thirteen thirty-two-gun frigates of the American navy. Langdon hired the best shipbuilder in Portsmouth, James Hackett, and appointed Thomas Thompson to oversee construction. Materials came from the New Hampshire forest. Once the keel was laid, it took two months to complete the ship, which was launched on May 21, 1776. The *New Hampshire Gazette* reported that "she is esteemed by all those who are judges that have seen her, to be one of the compleatest ships ever built in America." As evidence of how "compleat" a ship she was, on launching it took a mere "six minutes from the time she run, without the least hurt; and what is truly remarkable, not a single person met with the least accident in launching, tho' near five hundred men were employed and about her when run off." Once at anchor in the harbor, the frigate only required sails and guns before she could put to sea. The former were outfitted on the ship quickly, but the latter, the thirty-two guns, took more than a year to arrive, so that throughout the rest of 1776 and half of 1777 the *Raleigh* rode at anchor, awaiting action against the British. Finally in August 1777, the *Raleigh* took to sea with Thomas Thompson as her captain. Accompanied by the twenty-four-gun *Alfred*, Thompson captured a small British sloop that had lagged behind a British convoy, forced her captain to betray the ship-to-ship signals of the convoy and had the daring to sail into the convoy undetected and fire upon the brig *Druid*. Thereupon *Raleigh* escaped the pursuing British—at least for a time. In September 1778, under a different commander, the *Raleigh* was captured by two British frigates and outfitted for the Royal Navy.

A more famous Piscataqua vessel than the *Raleigh* was the eighteen-gun sloop *Ranger*, commanded by John Paul Jones. Langdon again commissioned the *Ranger* and oversaw her construction at his own ship-works on Badger Island, just across the river from Strawbery Banke. Master builder Hackett constructed the vessel under the overall guidance of Tobias Lear, Langdon's cousin. The *Ranger* was a small boat, a sloop designed to employ twenty guns, sleek and long, built for speed. Jones thought that the "*Ranger*, in the Opinion of every Person who has seen her is looked upon to be one of the best Cruizers in America.—She will be always able to Fight her Guns under a most excellent Cover; and no Vessel yet built was ever calculated for sailing faster, and making good Weather." Captain Jones, a bachelor and ladies' man, held social court at the widow Purcell's (the Lord House, now called the John Paul Jones house) from July to October 1777, while he awaited the outfitting of the ship. The *Ranger* had been completed and launched in May, but still lacked armaments, sails and supplies. Langdon was ultimately responsible for such provisions, but the haphazardness of war and competing aims of

Congress and private contractors resulted in five months' delay before *Ranger* could sail. Jones, arrogant and particular, believed that Langdon was inadequate for the job, complaining in a letter that Langdon "thinks himself my Master—and he, who was bred in a shop and hath been about a voyage or two at sea under a Nurse, had once the assurance to tell me that he knew as well as myself how to fit out, Govern and Fight a Ship of War!" Jones went shopping for food and supplies, spending money on livestock for provisions and sailors slops to outfit the men. The *Ranger* sailed with a crew of 150, which Jones recruited with mixed success, privateers (and the possibility of greater profit) being more appealing to sailors. Captain Jones, according to Sarah Orne Jewett,

> *gathered the ship's company of the Ranger from* [Piscataqua] *farms. Old people, who died not many years ago, remembered him as he walked on the wharves at Portsmouth, with his sword point scratching the ground; a little wasp of a fellow, with a temper like a blaze of the gunpowder whose smoke he loved. One can imagine him scrambling up the shore here to one of the old farm-houses, as short as a boy; but as tall as a grenadier, in his pride and dignity; and marching into the best room, in all the vainglory and persuasiveness of his uniform, to make sure of a good fellow whose looks he liked, and whom he promised to send home a gallant hero, with his sea-chest full of prize-money.*

The Lord House is famous for hosting John Paul Jones on several occasions while he awaited the construction and outfitting of his ships *Ranger* and *America*. *Courtesy of Benjamin Lawson.*

The officers of the ship were selected by Langdon to Jones's chagrin. They included the ship's surgeon, Ezra Green of Dover.

Dr. Green was a Harvard graduate, merchant, horticulturist and surgeon who had arrived at Dover in 1767 to establish his medical practice. His next-door neighbor, the Reverend Jeremy Belknap, arrived at Dover at the same time to take a position at the First Parish, where Green soon became a leader. The two men became fast friends, as they were both natives of Massachusetts, Harvard graduates, inquisitive and new to New Hampshire for reasons of career. Both men found Dover to be an outpost of civilization, with little cultured society and intellectual stimulation. Green, with Belknap's earnest support, tried in vain to encourage the importance of public education in Dover—a place that had no such opportunities for the young during the war. Both men were warm Patriots as well, Belknap supporting the cause from the pulpit, Green as a surgeon first with the army then the navy. Dr. Green volunteered as a surgeon to the American army shortly after the battle of Bunker Hill and was with the troops under General Richard Montgomery, which marched through northern New York, spanned Lake Champlain, attacked Montreal, then retreated in 1776 under the leadership of Durham's General John Sullivan. In a letter he wrote from Ticonderoga at the end of October 1776, Dr. Green asked a friend, Nathaniel Cooper of Dover, to see whether or not he could help him "get a berth as surgeon of a good continental ship or a privateer." A year later, having returned to Dover and recovered from a long period of sickness, Dr. Green joined the navy as surgeon of the sloop of war *Ranger*.

The *Ranger* set sail on November 1, 1777, en route to France, seeking prizes along the way. The voyage proceeded quickly for the first fortnight, with little of consequence occurring except for a violent thunderstorm. On the sixteenth, high seas broke the tiller, disabling navigation and the ship turned windward, close to capsizing. On the twenty-third they came upon a brig, the *Mary*, "laden with fruit and wine," out from Malaga in Spain and headed for England; the *Mary* was their first prize. Two days later another English brig, the *George*, with the same cargo from the same location became the second prize of the voyage. On December 2, arriving at France, the ship "ran in for the Land with a fine moderate Breeze, narrowly escap'd running on a Sand through want of a Pilot and arrived all in good spirits at Peanbeauf on the River Loire and came to anchor in the evening." While at port the *Ranger* was outfitted with new sails and a shortened main mast to make her more responsive at sea and was loaded with all the naval stores and munitions needed to support Jones's plan to attack English port cities.

During the month of April the *Ranger* coasted north along the French coast from Nantes to Brittany and the city of Brest, from which she crossed the English Channel to the Irish Sea, through which they cruised and attacked British shipping, raided the west coast of England, and defeated the twenty-gun HMS *Drake* in battle. Throughout Dr. Green practiced his craft of surgery, which was limited to administering purgatives to those with stomach troubles, dressing the wounds of those injured in battle, diagnosing diseases such as smallpox and quarantining those so identified, sending the ill of the *Ranger* and captured ships to hospitals ashore, and comforting the mortally wounded. The *Ranger* returned to the Piscataqua in October 1778, under the command of Thomas

Simpson, who had replaced John Paul Jones. Dr. Green stayed ashore for several months, during which time he married Susannah Hayes, then took to sea again on the *Ranger* in March 1779. He wrote his wife on March 12:

> *I never felt so uneasy on account of your absence. I pray we may not long be separated from each other, but as Providence seems to have pointed out this to me as a duty, I desire to pursue it cheerfully and with good courage, and I know you would not wish me to turn or look back; and I wish you all the happiness of this world and that to come.*

During several voyages under Simpson's command the *Ranger* successfully took numerous prizes, of which the officers and crew enjoyed a portion. After a cruise with the privateer *Alexander* in 1781, Green retired from war service, returned to Dover, turned over his medical practice to Jacob Kittredge and, with peace in 1783, became a merchant.

The largest ship produced by Piscataqua shipbuilders during the war was the seventy-four-gun *America*, which was built at Badger Island under the supervision of William Hackett. The construction of the ship was halted repeatedly because of lack of funds, workers and supplies, and was not completed until 1782. She was to be under the command of John Paul Jones, who again stayed in Portsmouth to oversee her construction and outfitting, but toward the end of the war Congress decided to make the *America* a present to France. She was launched in November 1782. Jeremy Belknap, who was present at the launching, wrote that it required two attempts to launch the ship.

> *The reason of her not going off was, in the carpenter's phrase, that she was too strait-laced…They had taken so much care to keep her from falling, that she could not move but about twelve feet, and all the hawsers, tackles, and screws that could be used were ineffectual. At the second attempt she was launched, and…she went off as easily and gently as a canoe.*

The Independent State of New Hampshire

Such an easy launch could not, unfortunately, be said of the new United States of America. The Treaty of Paris ending the war in 1783 brought recognition of U.S. independence but a host of problems. Challenging the residents of the Piscataqua Valley was the uncertainty of trade, since there was no central authority to exercise oversight, a continuing lack of gold and silver specie and consequent depreciation of paper money, issued without stable foundation by many states of the U.S. Confederation. Debtors especially believed that if New Hampshire joined other states in issuing paper to increase the circulation of money, all would benefit. As one writer noted in a July 1786, issue of the *New Hampshire Gazette*:

> *Seven states are now blessed with harmony, plenty and happiness. Worthy, industrious men can go to market with a penny in their pockets; their benevolent friends, the farmers,*

meet them half way with cheerfulness, and are as ready to receive as they to offer; now one greets the other with social benedictions, trade flourishes, agriculture increases, mutual confidence is restored, and harmony reigns triumphant. Elysian fields these! when contrasted with the bondage of the inhabitants of New-Hampshire; for "in the midst of life, thy are in death," death of the worst kind, penury and want of the common blessings of providence. How long, freemen of New-Hampshire, can ye bear the yoke of oppression!

A number of rabble-rousers formed themselves into a convention that drew up a petition for addressing the grievances of the population and sent it to the legislature at Exeter. When the latter body ignored the petition, the authors inflamed the passions of many farmers and debtors, mustered them at Kingston and marched in military order to Exeter, where they invaded the legislature and demanded at the point of a gun that the petition be considered. President John Sullivan refused, and the legislature attempted to carry on business as usual surrounded by loaded muskets of armed men. Toward evening, the insurgents lost their nerve and dispersed, promising to return the next day with the same demands. That evening, Sullivan called out the militia, and the next morning infantry and cavalry mustered and approached the insurgents, who fled in the face of such a force. The leaders were captured and tried on charges of treason and were sufficiently humbled and penitent that they were freed. In due course, the legislature took up the cause of paper money and decided against it.

The New Hampshire insurgency, as well as Shays' Rebellion in Massachusetts, were spurs to a movement in the thirteen states to create a stronger centralized government than that authorized by the Articles of Confederation. On March 3, 1787, President John Sullivan wrote Secretary of the Congress Charles Thomson that the New Hampshire General Court had voted to send delegates to Philadelphia as part of the overall plan (which was decided upon from the summer of 1786 to the winter of 1787) to send representatives from each state to decide on the future of the Confederation. Thomson wrote Sullivan that he had "the honor to inform you that your letter of the 3d of this month with the vote of the General court appointing Delegates to meet in Convention at Philadelphia has been duly received, & communicated to Congress." New Hampshire delegates included John Langdon of Portsmouth; they met and created the draft of a new government, the Constitution, which they sent to the thirteen states in September, suggesting that conventions be formed in each state to decide for or against the new government—if nine of the thirteen approved, the Constitution would be ratified. The New Hampshire convention met at Exeter, and in February 1788, approved the adoption of the Constitution as the ninth and deciding vote for ratification.

Politics among inhabitants of the Piscataqua were often heated, as some people, such as Colonel Joseph Whipple, wanted only the limited government of the Confederation, while others, such as John Sullivan, were heavily committed to a stronger government such as that offered by the Constitution. Whipple was a native of Kittery and brother of William Whipple, a signer of the Declaration of Independence.

This early twentieth century print of John Langdon's mansion shows the imposing entrance befitting one of Portsmouth's leading Patriots. *From* Vignettes of Portsmouth.

William Whipple Sr., a sailor and merchant, had moved to Kittery in the 1720s, where he married Mary Cutt, daughter of Kittery shipbuilder Robert Cutt. The newlyweds inherited land with a secure cove on the Piscataqua not far from the river's mouth, which subsequently became known as Whipple's Cove. There William Jr. was born in 1730, and Joseph in 1738. The brothers went to sea as merchants, following the path of their father, and having made a modest fortune retired to Portsmouth in 1759 to invest in shipping, allowing others to do the sailing. Both men served in the Revolutionary army, William as a general and Joseph as a colonel of the militia. Joseph became committed to limited government and became a staunch Anti-Federalist and Democratic-Republican in the late 1780s and 1790s. More conservative nationalists such as John Sullivan knew of Joseph Whipple's liberal support of the Confederation; Sullivan suspected and accused Whipple of using his office of collector of customs for Portsmouth for political purposes. The state in 1786 and 1787 was in financial difficulty, as gold and silver specie had been drained from state coffers during the war. Treasurer John Gilman scarcely had funds to pay salaries to public officials, who could, however, apply to Whipple for funds collected from customs. Some had, and they received payment from Whipple. Sullivan applied to Whipple and was refused, which made him suspect that Whipple was favoring those of his own political sympathies. If so, Whipple would no doubt have lost his position upon the inauguration of the Federalist George Washington in 1789. Washington, however, retained Whipple in the office, in which Whipple served until his death in 1816, having been absent from the position for a few years when Federalist John Adams was president. Whipple lived in a stately mansion on State Street in Portsmouth, which still stands.

PRESIDENTIAL PARADE

Upon the inauguration of the new government in 1789, President Washington determined that a tour of the states would be in order; he set out to visit the northern states in the fall of 1789, reaching New Hampshire on October 31. There he was greeted by New Hampshire dignitaries, including president of the state John Sullivan and U.S. senators John Langdon and Paine Wingate of Stratham. The president, according to the *New Hampshire Gazette*, "passed the troops drawn up to receive him; who severally vied with each other, who could pay the most respect to the man whom Heaven approves, and Americans delight to honour. The President then dismounted from his horse, took his carriage and was escorted to Greenland. The way, for the most part, being lined with spectators of all ranks." The entourage wound its way to Portsmouth through Hampton Falls, Hampton and Greenland. The citizens of New Hampshire, like those of Massachusetts and Connecticut, where the president had visited in October, lined the way to see the great man, with tears in their eyes and tremors in their voices. "At his entrance into this town," Portsmouth, the *Gazette* continued,

> he was saluted by thirteen Cannon from three companies of Artillery... The street through
> which he passed [Congress Street] was lined by the citizens of the town, all the crafts

being ranged alphabetically; the Bells rang a joyful peal, and repeated shouts from grateful thousands, hail'd their Deliverer welcome to the Metropolis of New-Hampshire…A federal Salute was fired from the Castle, the ships in the harbour were dressed, and the windows and doors of every house were crowded with ladies, anxious to see and bless the man to whom America stands so much indebted.

Washington was enthusiastically and elegantly entertained, toasted, sung to, painted and eulogized. He had tea with John Langdon; went fishing for cod off the shores of Kittery, followed by a barge of enthusiastic musicians playing tunes for the president to fish by; attended St. John's, the Anglican church, and North Parish, the Congregational church, where he heard a sermon directed more to Washington than to the divine by Joseph Buckminster; dined with John Sullivan at Stavers Tavern; and "in the evening, an elegant ball was given by the gentlemen of Portsmouth, which the President honoured with his presence, when he was introduced to a brilliant circle of more than seventy ladies." Exhausted from such adulation, Washington departed Portsmouth for the return trip, proceeding as quickly as possible through Stratham and Exeter, where he dined at Folsom's Tavern, before returning to Massachusetts.

The imposing entrance to Fort Constitution on Newcastle Island. *Courtesy of Benjamin Lawson.*

Stavers' Tavern, also called Earl of Halifax Tavern and William Pitt Tavern in the 1700s, hosted lively political debates during the Revolutionary War years. *Courtesy of Benjamin Lawson.*

Progress on the Piscataqua

The people of the Piscataqua Valley, as elsewhere in America, knew Washington to be the great hero of the war; he symbolized the American will to live free, the republican spirit that drove people to fight and die for their beliefs. The American Revolution for these people was literally a break from the past, a new beginning. This spirit of newness and movement into the future was concretely realized in numerous activities and institutions, some grand, others more modest. In Exeter, philanthropist John Phillips provided the determination and the funds to open a seminary of learning based on the humanistic models of the Renaissance and ancient Greece, Phillips Exeter Academy. Here students, according to Jeremy Belknap, were "taught the learned languages, the principles of geography, astronomy, mathematics, and logic; besides writing, music, composition and oratory. Particular attention is given to the morals of the students and their instruction in the principles of natural and revealed religion, and the exercises of piety and virtue." Not long after, Jonathan Hamilton, a wealthy merchant of Berwick, provided the funds to begin an academy of learning in that town, Berwick Academy. Hamilton, according to Sarah Orne Jewett, was

Initially called Queen's Chapel, St. John's Parish was home of the Anglican (Episcopal) community of Portsmouth. The current structure was built in 1807. *Courtesy of Benjamin Lawson.*

a shipowner and merchant, who from humble beginnings accumulated his great fortune in the West Indian trade. He was born on Pine Hill, in the northern part of the town; but built later the stately old house at the Lower Landing, and lived in it the rest of his life, with all the magnificence that was possible in his day. On his archaic looking tomb, in the Old Fields burying ground, the long high-sounding inscription ends with the solemn words, "Hamilton is no more."

Berwick Academy, like Phillips Exeter, focused on teaching the humanistic liberal arts to the young people of the Piscataqua Valley. Other Piscataqua towns, unable to create grand academies of learning, took initial steps toward the same goal with the creation of social libraries. Jeremy Belknap, for example, was instrumental in beginning the social library of Dover. The model for subsequent public libraries, the social library began with a few interested citizens contributing modest funds to buy books that could be circulated among them. The more people joined the association, the more books could be bought and the greater the variety of reading material for each member. Other Piscataqua residents expressed their republic spirit in public works. For example, shortly after the end of the Revolution, investors led by John Peirce built the Piscataqua Bridge spanning the narrow strait between Dover Point and Bloody Point in Newington. After the turn of the century other bridges would be built, notably to span the Piscataqua between Portsmouth and Kittery. The first was built in 1822. Eliphalet Ladd, native of Exeter and resident of Portsmouth, spearheaded a move to provide fresh water for a growing Portsmouth. He and other leaders of Portsmouth petitioned the New Hampshire legislature to allow the incorporation of the Portsmouth Aqueduct Company to construct an aqueduct to the town, "for the purpose of watering said Town," which will "be a lasting conveniency to the Inhabitants, and in case of fires would prove a great public benefit." The plan succeeded, and the aqueduct provided Portsmouth with fresh, plentiful water for generations.

Religion in the Piscataqua Valley

Other changes to the Piscataqua Valley brought about by the American Revolution were of a spiritual sort. Congregationalism, the Puritan way of the sixteenth and early seventeenth centuries, slowly gave way to pluralism in belief. In the colonial period all citizens, no matter their personal religious beliefs, were taxed a parish rate in support of the town pastor and church. Before the mid-eighteenth century, there were few alternatives to Congregationalism. Anglican (Episcopal) congregations were rare, and these tended to be wealthy and conservative—during the Revolution they were often Loyalists. St. John's in Portsmouth was Anglican, and some of its members, such as Theodore Atkinson, were Tory.

Religious changes occurred with the beginning of conflict in the 1760s. The Society of Friends (Quakers), once persecuted in seventeenth-century New Hampshire (though they lived without molestation at the same time in Maine), became bolder at the beginning of the eighteenth century, establishing societies in Dover, Kittery and Brentwood.

The elite of Portsmouth attended and were buried at St. John's Parish. Theodore Atkinson was a longtime Portsmouth leader and provincial counselor who stayed loyal to King George III during the Revolution. *Courtesy of Benjamin Lawson.*

The Dover society built a meetinghouse around 1700, and they enjoyed an increasing number of converts during the 1700s, to the chagrin of Congregational pastors such as Jeremy Belknap. The atmosphere of change that the Revolution encouraged in freedom of conscience helped nontraditional denominations, such as the Quakers and Baptists, grow. Baptist congregations began to flourish at the end of the eighteenth century; Exeter's Baptist society began in 1800, Portsmouth's in 1826; a Free Will Baptist congregation was organized at Dover in 1826. Various brands of liberal Christianity, for example Universalism, gained adherents in New Hampshire. Universalist preachers such as John Murray preached at Portsmouth in 1776, and a Universalist congregation was founded there at the close of the war. A Universalist congregation was established at Exeter in 1810, and Dover in 1825; a Unitarian church opened at Dover two years later. An obscure sect founded by John Glas of Scotland and promulgated by Robert Sandeman in America had adherents in the Piscataqua as well—there was a Sandemanian church in Portsmouth, for example, before the Revolution.

Religious conservatives who came to accept the rejection of divine wrath and belief that all souls will be joined with God in Heaven included Jeremy Belknap, pastor of the First Parish of Dover. During the Revolution Jeremy Belknap slowly changed from Calvinism to Universalism, as did his mentor Samuel Haven, minister of the South Parish, whose inclination toward a belief in universal salvation also grew in the 1770s and 1780s. He even named one of his sons Charles Chauncy in honor of the Boston minister and leading Universalist of the same name. Belknap did not go so far, but he did struggle with his beliefs, wondering how a God of goodness and justice could condemn his children to everlasting torment. The Revolution was not kind to Jeremy and his wife, the former Ruth Eliot of Boston. Belknap's parish of farmers, coopers, shipbuilders and sawyers struggled to make ends meet as the war progressed and prices rose. They became fearful, unwilling to risk change, afraid to part with their feeble savings, even in support of their spiritual leader Belknap. Jeremy and Ruth, who had long been friends in Boston before they married, followed the call of the clergy to the Piscataqua in 1767; husband and wife considered the Piscataqua, save perhaps for Portsmouth, as a frontier outpost of civilization. Jeremy missed the company of intellectuals like himself, which he rarely found in the Piscataqua Valley. He compensated by frequent trips to Boston and a constant correspondence with men of learning. Ruth missed the society of Boston, her many friends and family that remained in the city notwithstanding the British occupation at the beginning of the war. Like her husband, she turned to the pen for solace, composing a humorous poem in 1782 to express her disillusionment.

> *Dear Cousin,—It is now Thanksgiving Night, and I should be thankful indeed if I could call and spend the evening with you, or have some agreeable friend call in upon me, but as this cannot be, I must converse this way. I have had frequent opportunities to Boston this fall, but expect this will be the last for some time: therefore am willing to improve it. And I think for your amusement I will send you "The Pleasures of a Country Life," written when I had a true taste of them by having no maid.*

The Piscataqua During the Revolution

Up in the morning I must rise
Before I've time to rub my eyes,
With half-pin'd gown, unbuckled shoe,
I haste to milk my lowing cow.
But, Oh! It makes my heart to ake,
I have no bread till I can bake,
And then, alas! It makes me sputter,
For I must churn or have no butter.
The hogs with swill too I must serve;
For hogs must eat or men will starve.
Besides, my spouse can get no cloaths
Unless I much offend my nose.
For all that try it know it's true
There is no smell like colouring blue.
Then round the parish I must ride
And make enquiry far and wide
To find some girl that is a spinner,
Then hurry home to get my dinner.
If with romantic steps I stray
Around the fields and meadows gay,
The grass, besprinkled with the dews,
Will wet my feet and rot my shoes.
If on a mossy bank I sleep
Pismires and crickets o'er me creep,
Or near the purling rill am seen
There dire musquitos pierce my skin.
Yet such delights I seldom see
Confind to house and family.
All summer long I toil & sweat,
Blister my hands, and scold & fret.
And when the summer's work is o'er,
New toils arise from Autumn's store.
Corn must be husk'd and pork be kill'd,
The house with all confusion fill'd.
O could you see the grand display
Upon our annual butchering day,—
See me look like ten thousand sluts,
My kitchen spread with grease & guts,—
You'd lift your hands surpris'd, & swear
That Mother Trisket's self were there.
Yet starch'd up folks that live in town,
That lounge upon your beds till noon,
That never tire yourselves with work,
Unless with handling knife & fork,
Come, see the sweets of country life,
Display'd in Parson B------'s wife.

South Parish, Portsmouth. Built in the 1820s, this imposing granite structure hosts the Unitarian Universalist Society. *Courtesy of Benjamin Lawson.*

The North Parish, founded in 1712, was the second congregation formed in Portsmouth. The present structure dates from 1854. *Courtesy of Benjamin Lawson.*

At the same time some ministers and their congregations refused to alter their beliefs, and fiercely held on to traditional Puritanism. Joseph Buckminster, who became the pastor at North Parish in 1779, was a very conservative minister of the Gospel. Belknap was friends with Buckminster, whom he nicknamed "The Metropolitan." Belknap described Buckminster as "nervous to a high degree, has an excellent heart." Buckminster was also, apparently, a dreamer; he confided to Belknap in 1784 his idea respecting the new invention, the hot-air balloon, that "a very good use might be made of these air-balloons which are so much talked of, without endangering anybody's life or limbs," by propelling horseless carriages along city streets. Buckminster, who had married a local beauty, Eliza Stevens, daughter of Reverend Joseph Stevens of Kittery, was "an excellent husband, though sometimes rather too gloomy, which he cannot help"—Belknap thought Buckminster found the Piscataqua as confining as himself.

A unique religious expression in the Piscataqua Valley was the Shakers. "There are a few of them at Barrington" on the Ising-glass River, a tributary of the Cocheco, Belknap wrote, "about 6 or 7 miles from here…They have strange postures and actions; the common opinion is that they are under the power of *witchcraft*. This is the usual way (among ignorant people) of solving every uncommon appearance." The Shakers believed, according to Belknap, "that they are judges of the world, and that the dead are daily rising, and coming before them to be judged." Sinners such as George Fox (the founder of the Society of Friends) and George Whitefield (a leading preacher of the Great Awakening) appeared before the Shakers and were "absolved from their errors, and are now at rest."

FREE AT LAST

A significant consequence of the American Revolution was the end of slavery in New Hampshire. Slaves had first been brought to the Piscataqua in the mid-1600s; by the mid-1700s, there were close to two hundred; by 1776, close to three hundred. Unlike the agrarian South, where slavery was an economic institution, slavery existed in the Piscataqua Valley as a symbol of wealth and status. Particularly in Portsmouth, town leaders such as William Vaughan, Richard Wibird, John Langdon and William Whipple had slaves, especially males who served as domestic servants. John Sullivan of Durham had slaves. Even ministers, such as Reverend Joseph Stevens of Kittery, owned slaves. Piscataqua merchants did not engage in the slave trade, but imported slaves from the West Indies. An advertisement in the *New Hampshire Gazette* for October 10, 1760, read: "To be sold at the House of John Stavers, Innholder in Portsmouth next Wednesday at 3 o'clock, A few new negroes lately imported in Snow *General Townsend*, Monsieur Bunbury Commander, from the West Indies." The owner of the *Gazette*, Daniel Fowle, had a slave named Prime who served as the pressman. In August 1757, the *Gazette* ran an advertisement about an escaped slave Scipio, the "manservant" of James Dwyer. Scipio was described as *well sett, and of a yellowish Complexion; had on one of his Hands a Scar. Said Negro was born and brought up among the English; he understands Husbandry, mows well, and affects to be thought a Man of Sense. He had on, and carried with him when he Run away, a Saxon blue Frize Jacket with small Metal Buttons, Slash sleves lined with whites Bays, a brown Fustin Under Jacket without Sleves, scarlet Everlasting Breeches Yarn Stockings almost white, and one Wollen Check Shirt, and an odd Hat and Cap. Whoever shall apprehend said Runaway, or bring him to his said Master in Portsmouth aforesaid, or secure him so that he may have him again, shall have* TEN DOLLARS *Reward, and all necessary Char[g]es paid by James Dwyer. If the said Scipio will of his own Accord (without putting me to the Charge of the Above Reward) return home, he shall be kindly received, and have his Absconding forgiven.*

This abandoned slave cemetery is found on the grounds of Christ Episcopal Church in Portsmouth. *Photo by author.*

Anecdotal accounts explained the end of slavery in the Piscataqua due to brave slaves fighting for freedom in the Revolution and grateful masters realizing the absurdity of slavery in a land of liberty and manumitting them. The reality was that slaves were too expensive at a time when the economy suffered under inflation and declining trade. Slavery declined in New Hampshire not because of law—there never was a law outlawing the *peculiar institution*—rather because the Revolution changed the economic and institutional climate of the Piscataqua, and it was no longer tenable. Among his contemporaries, Belknap was rare in his lifelong opposition to slavery and willingness to treat African Americans with equality.

Contemporaries such as Jeremy Belknap believed, with the ratification of the Constitution in 1788 and the establishment of government in 1789 under the leadership of President George Washington, that "the American revolution appears to be completed." Belknap ended his *History of New-Hampshire* with the prayer that "harmony may prevail between the general government, and the jurisdiction of each state, as the peculiar delicacy of their connexion requires; and that the blessings of 'peace, liberty, and safety,' so dearly obtained, may descend inviolate to our posterity."

CHAPTER FIVE
THE AGE OF SAIL

Ship building" on the Piscataqua, Jeremy Belknap wrote in the *History of New-Hampshire*,

> *has always been a considerable branch of business. European traders often came hither to build ships, which they could do much cheaper than at home, by the profit made on the goods, which they brought with them. Our own merchants also built ships of two and three hundred tons; which were employed in voyages, to the British sugar islands, with a lading of lumber, fish, oil, and live stock.*

Piscataqua shipbuilders built a number of notable war vessels during the wars of the seventeenth and eighteenth centuries, such as the *Faukland*, fifty-four guns (1690), the *Bedford*, thirty-two guns (1696), the *America*, forty guns (1749), as well as the *Raleigh*, *Ranger* and *America* during the Revolution. Shipbuilding extended to the tributaries of the Piscataqua: the Newichawannock, Cocheco, Lamprey, Oyster and Squamscot.

> *Such operations are generally set up on the banks of the river, but sometimes vessels of an hundreds [sic] tons and upwards, have been built at the distance of one or two miles from the water, and drawn on strong sledges of timber, on the snow, by teams of two hundred oxen, and placed on the ice of the rivers so as to float in the spring. They have also been built at the distance of seven or eight miles; then taken to pieces, and conveyed in common team loads to the sea. Fishing schooners and whale-boats are often built at the distance of two or three miles from the water.*

When he wrote volume three of the *History of New-Hampshire* in 1792, Belknap reported that eight ships were built in 1790 and twenty in 1791. This increase mirrored an expansion in Piscataqua trade during the 1790s. Overall in 1791, there were eighty-three vessels working on the Piscataqua and its tributaries. During the years before the war, the number of vessels clearing port with exports and entering port with imports was well over three hundred per year. Much of the trade was coastal or to places in the British Empire, especially the West Indies. After the Revolution, trade with other European countries, such as France and Spain, increased, as well as trade in the East Indies. Fishing shallops and schooners departed port every day. Belknap reported that in 1791 there were forty-seven boats totaling 630 tons and 250 mariners involved in the Piscataqua fishery. Eliphalet Ladd was one of the leading Piscataqua shipbuilders after the War for Independence. A native of Exeter who relocated to Portsmouth in the 1790s, he was builder of the five-hundred-ton *Hercules*, a merchant ship engaged in the East Indies trade. James Hackett continued his shipbuilding activities as well, building such ships as the thirty-six-gun *Congress*, which was part of the new postwar American navy.

Washington, on his visit to the Piscataqua in 1789, had made note of the deep-water harbors, numerous islands and narrow, swift channels of the river, which combined with the longstanding shipbuilding tradition made the Piscataqua a likely place for a U.S. Navy shipyard. The federal government purchased Seavey's Island adjacent to Kittery in 1800. By the time Nathaniel Adams penned the *Annals of Portsmouth* in the 1820s, the "Navy Yard" had several

> buildings for the accommodation of the officers and men; two ship houses sufficiently extensive to cover the largest ships employed in the Navy, and a Dock Yard for the preservation of timber. This island contains upwards of fifty-eight acres, and cost five thousand five hundred dollars. Besides the carpenters, smiths and labourers employed in the yard, a company of marines is stationed here as a guard. A distinguished officer of the Navy has usually had the command at this station.

About the same time the site of Fort William and Mary, taken over by the United States, was rebuilt and refortified. The old lighthouse, built in 1771, was replaced by a new wooden lighthouse during the Jefferson administration. Walls were enlarged and buildings for powder and troops constructed. Across the Piscataqua, the United States acquired land on Kittery Point where the old Pepperrell fort existed, and fortified it with huge granite blocks, powder houses, barracks and batteries that featured small artillery.

Piscataqua Politics

The Piscataqua communities, focused on maritime affairs, were necessarily involved in international trade and politics. Upon the end of the War for Independence and the Treaty of Paris, the new United States of America had to deal as an equal with European powers. Rivalries about trade and fishing often spilled over into naval conflict. The United States stood for freedom of the seas and free trade, but European events threatened to negate this stand. After the French Revolution began in 1789, for example, which resulted in a violent conflict with monarchist English that lasted until 1815, the American perception of freedom of the seas was starkly rejected by English as well as French vessels, which arbitrarily stopped and searched American vessels. English ships often discovered deserters from the Royal Navy aboard American ships and impressed them back into the Royal Navy, and some American seamen were mistaken for British sailors. The American government protested the manhandling of American ships, but as the British had the largest navy in the world, Americans often felt helpless to back up protests with retaliation. One technique, nonimportation of British goods—used to oppose the British in the years before the Revolution—was reinstated, particularly during the Jefferson administration. Indeed, a full embargo against the British and French was enacted by Congress in 1807, to the impairment of American trade. The growing conflict between the Americans and English eventually resulted in the War of 1812.

The Piscataqua and Fort Constitution form the background in this photograph of the entrance of a caponier at Fort McClary, which housed marksmen to defend the fort at the river shore. *Courtesy of Benjamin Lawson.*

The rifleman's house, one of three standing structures at Fort McClary, was built in the 1840s. *Courtesy of Benjamin Lawson.*

During the 1790s and early 1800s, there were two political factions that dominated politics in America—the Federalists and the Democratic-Republicans. The latter was primarily an agrarian, Southern-oriented faction, while the Federalists had more support from urban, mercantile regions, especially in the Northeast. Piscataqua towns, focused on trade and shipbuilding, were dominantly Federalist. The Federalist Party weakened, however, in the early 1800s during the Democratic-Republican administrations of Thomas Jefferson (1801–09) and James Madison (1809–17). Federalists, particularly in Massachusetts, pushed for unified opposition against the policies of Jefferson and Madison. Daniel Webster, a young lawyer living in Portsmouth, became a leading

Federalist in New Hampshire and was elected to the House of Representatives in 1812, where he was a leader of the small opposition to Madison's policies and the War of 1812. Some Federalists sought to secede from the Union over the issues of trade and war and met in the Hartford Convention, but Webster was not one of them. Nor did Webster abandon the Federalist cause during the Jefferson-Madison years, as did some of his Congressional colleagues, including Nicholas Gilman of Exeter and John Langdon of Portsmouth. Gilman, a veteran of the Revolutionary War and delegate to the New Hampshire convention to ratify the Constitution, served as a Federalist in the House of Representatives for four terms in the 1790s, during the administrations of Presidents Washington and Adams. He was elected to the U.S. Senate in 1804, this time as a Democratic-Republican. Likewise, John Langdon served as a Federalist for two terms in the U.S. Senate from 1789 to 1801, but in the early 1800s served in the state legislature and as governor as a Democratic-Republican. Gilman and Langdon had been intrigued by the economic policies of Secretary of the Treasury Alexander Hamilton, the leading Federalist of the 1790s. But after Hamilton's fall from power and death, the Federalist Party declined in power, and many statesmen joined ranks with the Democratic-Republicans.

The two political parties, the Federalists and Democratic-Republicans, were divided in their support of the British and French. No matter, because the two great European powers at war would stop at nothing to hinder enemy trade. Most often, Piscataqua vessels going toward or leaving French ports were stopped by British war frigates; often their cargoes were confiscated. Piscataqua merchants and seamen had a tough choice to make: to oppose the British by the partial or complete cessation of trade would hurt the local economy, but to stand by while British warships violated American sovereignty and human rights was intolerable. Colonel Joseph Whipple saw both sides in his position as collector of customs. On the one hand, Piscataqua trade declined significantly. Whipple collected customs of $143,000 in 1800, but only $20,000 in 1808, after the embargo was enacted. Exports from the Piscataqua declined precipitously. At the same time, after 1807, Whipple's job was to order the cutter *New Hampshire* to cruise the mouth of the Piscataqua enforcing the embargo, halting and impounding Piscataqua vessels attempting to trade with the French. One of Whipple's duties, ironically, was the certification of seamen aboard Piscataqua vessels as American citizens, born and bred on the Piscataqua. Whipple certified, for example, in July 1807 (as quoted in Saltonstall's *Ports of Piscataqua*)

> *that Nathan'l Lear, Jr., an American Seaman, aged 16, or thereabouts, of the height of about 5 feet one inch, light complexion, brown hair, blue eyes, freckled in the face, has a natural mark of a brown colour below the breast on the left side, was born in Newcastle, N. H., has this day produced to me proof in the manner directed in the Act, intitled, 'An Act for the Relief & Protection of American Seamen,' and pursuant to the said Act, I do hereby certify that the said Nath. Lear, Junr. is a citizen of the U. S. of America.*

The blockhouse at Fort McClary, dating from the 1840s, featured three floors, connected by narrow stairwells; the top floor served as barracks. *Courtesy of Benjamin Lawson.*

"Mr. Madison's War," as the War of 1812 was sometimes derided in New England, was not popular in New Hampshire. Facing the hundreds of British war frigates were the half-dozen frigates of the U.S. Navy. As during the Revolution, the outnumbered warships as well as the cessation of trade with Britain was a blow to the local economy that required a response, which was the same as a generation earlier in the first conflict with Great Britain: Piscataqua merchants and seamen turned to privateering. Piscataqua privateers, the most famous of which were *Portsmouth* and *Fox*, captured hundreds of prizes during the war. The brigantine *Portsmouth*, called a "she-devil," set sail in 1814 and brought back such prizes as the *James*, which was loaded with "rum, gin, brandy, powder, tea, glass, printing-presses, nuts, pickles, mustard, and fish sauce." *Fox* was an extremely successful privateer. At sea for long periods of time throughout the war, *Fox* repeatedly brought in prizes worth hundreds of thousands of dollars. She sailed off the coast of Newfoundland and Nova Scotia, tempting fate, as British frigates heavily patrolled those waters. *Fox* came into contact with many warships, but outsailed every one and was never captured, being a "prime sailer," in the words of one local salt. Once, for example, off the coast of Halifax, she approached a ship that appeared at first to be a potential prize but turned out to be a warship, *Rifleman*, in disguise. *Fox*, carrying only thirteen guns, was no match for a British man-of-war and quickly fled with *Rifleman* in pursuit. As quoted in Saltonsall,

The massive walls of Fort Constitution were made of large blocks of New Hampshire granite. *Courtesy of Benjamin Lawson.*

"We kept the Fox *a good full and beat dead to windward," recalled one sailor, "and by means of laying so much nearer the wind, were soon a good distance to windward of him. I will here remark that a schooner that will lay within five points of the wind and sail five knots per hour, in short tacks beating to windward, will beat any frigate in the British Navy."*

Such was what occurred, and *Fox* escaped *Rifleman*.

Fort Constitution was fortified to protect the Piscataqua in the years leading up to the war. The stone wall was expanded, powder magazines constructed and guns put into place. After the war began, when the British navy blockaded the American coast in 1814, the Americans responded by building a brick tower (called the Walbach Tower) upon which to mount a thirty-two-pound gun. After the war, Fort Constitution continued to provide defenses and was again fortified when the Civil War began. Huge one-hundred-pound Parrott Rifles (invented by New Hampshire native Robert Parrott) were put in place to guard the mouth of the river and harbor. Across the river Fort McClary, fortified in 1844 with an imposing blockhouse, received thirty-two-pound guns during the Civil War.

The U.S. Navy turned out frigates during the War of 1812 and Civil War. One, the seventy-four-gun man-of-war *Washington*, was built at the Portsmouth Naval Shipyard under the supervision of Isaac Hull. Captain Hull, who took charge of the shipyard in 1813, had recently gained fame for commanding the USS *Constitution* in the famous battle with HMS *Gurriere*, in which the victorious *Constitution* had been nicknamed *Old Ironsides*. As commander of the shipyard, Hull oversaw its expansion in labor and facilities, including the construction of a massive shiphouse named after Benjamin Franklin. Here the *Washington* was constructed, though it took so long that the ship never saw action in the war. In subsequent years, the shipyard turned out the USS *Portsmouth* in 1843, a thousand-ton ship that participated in the Mexican War, and later the USS *Kearsarge*, equipped with steam and sails, which fought during the Civil War. Launched right at the end of the Civil War was the USS *Agamenticus*, an ironclad, which never saw military action. The shipyard at midcentury also repaired ships such as the USS *Franklin*, a seventy-four-gun frigate that was outfitted with steam at the shipyard, and *Old Ironsides* (the USS *Constitution*) which received needed repairs in 1855.

Meanwhile, Piscataqua shipbuilders turned out long and lean clipper ships in the mid-1800s. Two shipyards of note were the Fernald and Pettigrew yard on Badger's Island and the Raynes yard near the North Mill Pond. Fernald and Pettigrew built such ships as the *Typhoon*, which recorded one of the fastest Atlantic crossings under sail when in 1851 it sailed from Portsmouth to Liverpool in a little over thirteen days. Raynes built clippers such as *Witch of the Waves*, a fifteen-hundred-ton ship used in the East India trade, sailing down the coast of America around Cape Horn through Pacific waters to Asian ports. Clipper ships were eclipsed by steam-driven ironclads during and after the Civil War.

The magazine at Fort Constitution protected the black powder used in the massive guns that defended the Piscataqua. *Courtesy of Benjamin Lawson.*

The artillery pintles of Fort Constitution once held one-hundred-pound Parrott Rifles. *Photo by Benjamin Lawson.*

The USS *Portsmouth* was a twenty-four-gun sloop of war, built in the 1840s at the Portsmouth Naval Shipyard. *Courtesy of Benjamin Lawson.*

USS. Portsmouth

Tugboats are frequently seen moored next to the varied wharves adjacent to the many shops and restaurants of Portsmouth. *Courtesy of Benjamin Lawson.*

The gundalow was the workhorse of river transport on the Piscataqua River from the 1700s to the 1900s. *Courtesy of Benjamin Lawson.*

Piscataqua River trade was carried on by smaller boats, such as packets and gundalows, during the 1800s. Packets were small sailing craft that could sail the shallow waters of the Salmon Falls, Cocheco, Oyster, Lamprey and Squamscot, carrying cargo and passengers from Portsmouth and Kittery upriver to Exeter, Newmarket, Durham, Dover, Berwick and Eliot, a new town in 1810, once part of Kittery. Packets along with gundalows were important conveyors of cotton upriver to Piscataqua factories and finished goods downriver to Portsmouth for overseas export.

One of the most common sites on the Piscataqua during the Age of Sail was the gundalow under sail, negotiating the currents of the river and its tributaries, loaded to the hilt with cords of wood, bricks, granite and foodstuffs, connecting the towns and ports of the Piscataqua Basin. Gundalows first appeared on the Piscataqua in the 1600s: they were barges without sails, deck or rudder propelled by the current and long poles. By the 1700s they featured rudder, deck and square sail for more effective propulsion. During the 1800s, gundalow builders introduced a triangular lateen sail in the bow of the boat. The gundalow held up to fifty tons and could be up to seventy feet long. Sarah Orne Jewett recalled gundalows sailing about the waters of the Piscataqua basin in the mid-1800s:

Jacob Sheafe's warehouse on the Piscataqua River is over three hundred years old and is presently located at Prescott Park in Portsmouth. *Courtesy of Benjamin Lawson.*

In this house, located at Strawbery Banke, Thomas Bailey Aldrich spent several childhood years, which became the basis for his novel *Story of a Bad Boy*. *Courtesy of Benjamin Lawson.*

Even so lately as forty years ago there was a picturesque fleet of twenty gundalows with lateen sails, sailing from the Landing wharves to Portsmouth, beside a good-sized packet boat which went every other day. We know so little of the ways of the people a hundred or two hundred years ago, that it is a pleasure to be able to recall the customs of only fifty years since, and to be able to picture to ourselves, not only the people, but the way they lived in their pleasant houses and spent their time in the same pleasant houses and along the quiet streets that we ourselves know. When you see the last of the gundalows coming up the river, you will like to remember that its ancestor was copied from a Nile boat, from which a sensible old sea captain once took his lesson in shipbuilding. The high peaked sail looks like a great bird's wing, and catches the flawy wind well in the river reaches.

Towns along the fall line such as Berwick and Dover were centers of the lumber industry, which kept the gundalows busy taking loads of wood back and forth from the upper to the lower Piscataqua. As Jewett noted,

The northern country was covered…for the most part, with heavy pine growth; and the chief business at Berwick was buying this from the lumbermen, and sending it to Portsmouth, there to be reshipped, or direct to the West Indies, where the usual course of the ships was to load with rum, tobacco and molasses, and then to Russia where this second cargo was exchanged for iron, duck and cordage, then back to Liverpool for another trade, and so home. The little ships made money fast enough, and in the winter time the Berwick streets were crowded with ox teams and huge timber pines and piles of plank and boards. Sometimes gangs of teamsters, with their oxen, came in great companies from the White Mountains, and even from Vermont through the Crawford Notch.

By the end of the 1800s, the significance of the Piscataqua in American maritime history began to wane. Observers, such as writer Thomas Bailey Aldrich, who grew up in Portsmouth and recurrently returned to the city, saw the Piscataqua as a place to paint, write and sing about, a place of rich history if uncertain future. Aldrich's writings expressed a sense of the imagery and beauty if not dynamism of Portsmouth and the Piscataqua.

PISCATAQUA RIVER
Thou singest by the gleaming isles,
By woods, and fields of corn,
Thou singest, and the sunlight smiles
Upon my birthday morn.
But I within a city, I,
So full of vague unrest,
Would almost give my life to lie
An hour upon thy breast.
To let the wherry listless go,
And, wrapt in dreamy joy,

The Age of Sail

Dip, and surge idly to and fro,
Like the red harbor-buoy;
To sit in happy indolence,
To rest upon the oars,
And catch the heavy earthy scents
That blow from summer shores;
To see the rounded sun go down,
And with its parting fires
Light up the windows of the town
And burn the tapering spires;
And then to hear the muffled tolls
From steeples slim and white,
And watch, among the Isles of Shoals,
The Beacon's orange light.
O River! flowing to the main
Through woods, and fields of corn,
Hear thou my longing and my pain
This sunny birthday morn;
And take this song which fancy shapes
To music like thine own,
And sing it to the cliffs and capes
And crags where I am known!

Aldrich's poem prefaces his *An Old Town by the Sea*, published in 1883. As a boy he lived for a time in Portsmouth, experiences that became the basis for his novel *Story of a Bad Boy*. He was a well-known writer and editor of the *Atlantic Monthly* when he spent summers at the Piscataqua in the late 1880s. He commented on the changes to Portsmouth that, for someone seeking repose, were not entirely unwelcome:

What a slumberous, delightful, lazy place it is! The sunshine seems to lie a foot deep on the planks of the dusty wharf, which yields up to the warmth a vague perfume of the cargoes of rum, molasses, and spice that used to be piled upon it. The river is as blue as the inside of a harebell. The opposite shore, in the strangely shifting magic lights of sky and water, stretches along like the silvery coast of fairyland. Directly opposite you is the navy yard, and its neat officers' quarters and workshops and arsenals, and its vast shiphouses, in which the keel of many a famous frigate has been laid. Those monster buildings on the water's edge, with their roofs pierced with innumerable little windows, which blink like eyes in the sunlight, and the shiphouses. On your right lies a cluster of small islands,—there are a dozen or more in the harbor—on the most extensive of which you see the fading-away remains of some earthworks thrown up in 1812. Between this—Trefethren's Island—and Peirce's Island lie the Narrows. Perhaps a bark or a sloop-of-war is making up to town; the hulk is hidden among the islands, and the topmasts have the effect of sweeping across the dry land. On your left is a long bridge, more than a quarter of a mile in length, set upon piles where the water is twenty or thirty feet deep, leading to the navy yard and Kittery...This is a mere outline of the landscape that spreads before you. Its changeful beauty of form and color, with the summer clouds floating over it, is not to be painted in words. I know of many a place where the scenery is more varied and striking; but there is a mandragora quality in the atmosphere here that holds you to the spot, and makes the half-hours seem like minutes. I could fancy a man sitting on the end of that old wharf very contentedly for two or three years, provided it could be always in June.

Newspaperman Charles Brewster, Portsmouth resident and author of *Rambles About Portsmouth*, likewise wrote about the changes that had occurred by the mid-nineteenth century in Portsmouth:

At the present day we do not see the busy wharves, the fleets of West Indiamen, the great piles of bags of coffee, and the acres of hogsheads of molasses which we used to see; nor do we see Water street crowded with sailors, and the piles of lumber and cases of fish going on board the West Indiamen for uses in the Tropics.

Aldrich echoed these remarks, stating that

though many of the old landmarks have been swept away by the fateful hand of time and fire, the town impresses you as a very old town, especially as you saunter along the streets down by the river. The worm-eaten wharves, some of them covered by a sparse, unhealthy beard of grass, and the weather-stained, unoccupied warehouses are sufficient to satisfy a moderate appetite for antiquity. These deserted piers and these long rows of empty barracks, with their sarcastic cranes projecting from the eaves, rather puzzle the stranger. Why this great preparation for a commercial activity that does not exist, and evidently has not for years existed? There are no ships lying at the pier-heads; there are no gangs of stevedores staggering under heavy cases of merchandise; here and there is a barge laden down to the bulwarks with coal, and here and there a square-rigged schooner from Maine smothered with fragrant planks and clapboards; an imported citizen is fishing at the end of the wharf...in perfect sympathy with the indolent sunshine that seems to be sole proprietor of these crumbling piles and ridiculous warehouses, from which even the ghost of prosperity has flown

America had long been dependent upon the water routes for trade, travel and communication. During the Industrial Revolution of the nineteenth century, however, and the increasing use of the railroad, land routes became important for conveying goods. Railroads came to the Piscataqua in the 1840s, bringing goods to and from burgeoning factories at Portsmouth, Dover and Newmarket, relocating the focus of trade away from the Great Bay, Piscataqua and the harbor, to the iron rails that crossed the landscape, and the smokestacks that belched the symbol of American industry. Some Piscataqua towns, like Exeter, were reluctant to embrace industrialization and leave behind the past. The falls of the Squamscot provided some power to a variety of mills, but the great factories of other Piscataqua towns never appeared at Exeter. Shipbuilding declined in Exeter by the mid-1800s. At the same time the Oyster River was hardly large enough to provide significant power to factories in Durham, which appeared to be a declining town until resident Ben Thompson left his estate to New Hampshire to develop higher education; in the 1890s the New Hampshire College of Agricultural and Mechanic Arts (University of New Hampshire) was moved from Hanover to Durham, which became a college town.

Piscataqua towns such as Somersworth, Rollingsford, Dover and Newmarket built their future upon the Industrial Revolution. The Salmon Falls River provided power to a number of large factories built at Somersworth and Rollingsford, which split from Somersworth in 1849. The Salmon Falls Manufacturing Company was founded in 1822, in what became Rollingsford, the same year that the Great Falls Manufacturing Company was founded in Somersworth (called for many years Great Falls). These companies dominated the towns. Series of buildings and mills lined the water, with workers' houses nearby in long rows of sameness. As quoted in Clark and Faucher's *Around Somersworth*, one European traveler who visited Somersworth in 1840 wrote,

> *This is one of the pleasantest and most beautiful manufacturing villages…Along the outside of the main street are the boarding houses or dwelling houses for the mill workers; these are neat brick buildings, three stories in height, and each building contains four tenements: there are seven of these boarding houses, set at equal distance from each other, which gives to the whole an appearance of neatness and uniformity. The main street, the canal, and the mills, are running in parallel lines with a large open area between them, and have a most delightful effect upon the mind of a stranger when he first enters the village. The whole plan of the village displays good taste, and its general appearance is delightful and beautiful in the highest degree.*

The Great Falls Manufacturing Company strictly regulated the work, behavior and lifestyle of workers. The printed company regulations, as quoted in *Around Somersworth*, stated:

> *All persons in the employ of the Great Falls Manufacturing Company are requested to be punctual and constant in their attendance during the hours of labor and not to be absent from work without consent, excepting in cases of sickness, and then immediate information is to be sent to the overseer…All persons in the employ of the Company are positively required to abstain from the use of ardent spirits as a beverage. Profanity and indecent language cannot be permitted in the mills. All persons in the employ of this Company are earnestly advised to attend public worship on the Sabbath. Any person guilty or believed to be guilty of immoral, improper, or disorderly conduct, will be discharged.*

Tugboats are the modern workhorses of Portsmouth harbor, frequently seen plowing through the waters of the Piscataqua, often toward the mouth, to convey a waiting tanker to port. *Courtesy of Benjamin Lawson.*

Piscataqua towns became early leaders of the Industrial Revolution in America. The Cocheco Manufacturing Company, situated on the falls in Dover, was originally founded in 1812 as the Dover Cotton Factory. Like other industrial sites, immigrants from northern, southern and eastern Europe and Canada came to such Piscataqua factories looking for work. The Cocheco Manufacturing Company led Dover to become at one point in the nineteenth century one of the world leaders in textile manufacturing. The company owned a series of buildings along the Cocheco that produced cotton and calico. Local historian Samuel Stevens described the factory in 1833:

> *The principal manufacture is fine cotton cloth, No. 40, for calicoes, which are bleached and printed on the spot. No. 18, sheeting and No. 30, shirting also are made. The number of people employed in these three cotton mills, machine shops and calico printing establishments, is 800 females and 300 men and boys. These mills consume about 2600 Bales of Cotton, and turn out four and a half millions yards of cloth annually, or about 15,000 yards daily. The calico works make into fine Prints and Dyed Goods, (coloured Cambrics) 2500 pieces of 28 yards each, or 70,000 yards per week.*

Dover in 1833, according to Stevens, had, "exclusive of the works of the Cocheco Manufacturing Company":

> *1 Court House, 1 Jail, 1 Academy, 7 Meeting Houses, 7 Taverns, 9 School Houses, 2 Banks, 3 Printing Offices, 45 E[ast] and W[est] I[ndies] Goods Stores, 12 Provision and Retail Groceries, 5 Apothecaries, 2 Hard Ware Stores, 1 Crockery and Glass Ware Store, 2 Hat Stores, 1 Clothes and Drapery Store, 3 Bookstores, 2 Bookbinderies, 2 Circulating Libraries, 2 Social Libraries, 13 Shoe Stores and Manufactories, 5 Tanneries, 4 Saddle and Harness makers, 1 Carriage and Harness Manufactory, 1 Distillery, 3 Tin Ware Manufactories, 1 Iron Foundery, 8 Blacksmith shops, 2 Cabinet Warehouses, 2 Bake Houses, 1 Tallow Chandlery, 1 Flannel Manufactory, 4 Carding Machines, 5 Fulling Mills, 3 Saw Mills, 4 Grist Mills, 7 Tailor shops, 2 Slaughter Houses, 2 Reed Manufactories.*

Up the Cocheco River at Rochester and farther north at Farmington, factories were established for manufacturing shoes. In 1822 the Newmarket Manufacturing Company was founded at the lower falls of the Lamprey River. A series of granite mill buildings devoted to cotton textile manufacturing grew over the years. Eventually Newmarket boasted the largest factory (weaving) room in the world. Portsmouth also featured large factories, such as the Portsmouth Steam Factory, established in the 1840s to produce cotton fabrics, employing up to four hundred workers.

CONCLUSION

Sarah Orne Jewett, in her *Old Town of Berwick*, recorded a hilltop perspective of the forests and hills that the Piscataqua and tributaries, such as the Newichawannock, drain. "From the hilltop" of Powder House Hill, she wrote,

> which is high and bare like a Yorkshire moor, the eye follows a great procession of the New Hampshire mountains along the horizon from Saddleback to Mount Washington. If you look eastward you have a sense of being at the door of the great forests of Maine—a dark, pine-clad region stretches over and beyond Agamenticus. This way you are reminded of the loneliness that the settlers found, and westward you discover the smiling country of towns and farms that they began to build.

There are few mountains that hem in the Piscataqua, though to the northwest the massive White Mountain chain stands as a beacon on sunny winter days when the highest peaks, such as Mount Washington, shine. The White Mountains caught the attention of mariners cruising along the New Hampshire and Maine coast in the 1500s and 1600s, and attracted adventures such as Darby Field of Exeter, who journeyed thither in the 1640s. Residents of the Piscataqua Valley, as the years passed, grew so familiar with the distant, daunting presence of the White Mountains, the cold north wind that descended from snowy peaks, the rain clouds that formed among the peaks then made their way south and east to river valleys, the tales of wonder, mystery and the supernatural phenomena of the mountains that were told and retold over the decades, that some Piscataqua residents could not help but seek to know the mountains with the familiarity acquired by personal experience. Notable in this regard was Major Robert Rogers, the conqueror of the St. Francis Indians during the French and Indian War, who was the husband of Elizabeth Browne, daughter of Reverend Arthur Browne, rector of St. John's in Portsmouth. Rogers tried to ascend the Great Mountain (Mount Washington) but failed, the height and weather overcoming his courage and strength. Governor John Wentworth, who was something of a scientist and explorer, and had founded a landed estate at the town of Wolfeborough, north of the Piscataqua Valley adjacent to Lake Winnipesaukee, journeyed north to the White Mountains in 1772, ascending one or more of the highest peaks. Wentworth enthusiastically encouraged others to journey north; he hoped that enough travelers would seek to penetrate the mountain wilderness that towns would be founded and roads built. Wilderness roads were begun during his administration, which brought other explorers and settlers, such as Joseph Whipple of Portsmouth. Whipple became the sole proprietor of a township north of the White Mountains, which he christened Dartmouth (later renamed Jefferson). Whipple made numerous journeys between Portsmouth and Dartmouth, going usually through the Crawford Notch, sometimes the Pinkham Notch. Other scientists and adventurers sought to make the journey. Reverend Joseph Haven of Rochester vicariously explored the mountains every day, keeping a journal of the meteorological appearance and activity of the largest, Mount Washington. John Sullivan of Durham, who had grown up in the Piscataqua Valley, wished to journey to the White Mountains even if time and political duties prevented him. If he did not explore the mountains, he at least read about them enough to make himself, he thought, something of an expert. In a 1780 letter to a French scientist and diplomat staying in Philadelphia, Monsieur Marbois, Sullivan provided an inaccurate, absurd description at which, after asking to borrow and transcribe it, Jeremy Belknap laughed with fellow scientists who knew better. Belknap, who gained more knowledge than any of his contemporaries about the natural and human history of the White Mountains, wished to journey to the mountains as early as the 1760s. Not until the end of the Revolution, however, did Belknap journey to the mountains, accompanied by other Piscataqua residents—Joseph Whipple, and George Place and Enoch Wingate of Rochester, who served as guides to the expedition of clergymen, scientists, students and adventurers who explored the White Mountains, and ascended the Great Mountain (Mount Washington) in the summer of 1784.

Belknap, who had the heart (if not the physique) of an explorer, explored the hills and valleys of the Piscataqua when time and occasion offered. In 1782 he ascended the Salmon Falls River to near its source, and climbed Moose Mountain; about the same time he ascended a small mountain north of the Piscataqua called Agamenticus. One local tradition claimed that an elderly Passaconaway, chief of the Penacooks, ascended Agamenticus and, a recent Christian convert, preached to his followers. From its height Jeremy Belknap viewed

> *a most enchanting prospect. The cultivated parts of the country, especially on the south and south-west, appears as a beautiful garden, intersected by the majestick river Piscataqua, its bays and branches. The immense ranges of mountains on the north and north-west afford a sublime spectacle; and on the sea-side the various indentings of the coast from Cape Ann to Cape Elizabeth are plainly in view in a clear day; and the wide Atlantick stretches to the east as far as the power of vision extends.*

Conclusion

This early twentieth-century print shows the Portsmouth waterfront; the steeple of St. John's Episcopal Church soars above the town. *From* Vignettes of Portsmouth. *Courtesy of Benjamin Lawson.*

Cannon barrels once peered ominously from gun turrets at Fort Constitution. *Courtesy of Benjamin Lawson.*

Fort McClary served as the northern defense of the mouth of the Piscataqua River from the colonial period to the Spanish-American War. *Courtesy of Benjamin Lawson.*

The Piscataqua Valley looks remarkably similar today as it did over two hundred years ago in Belknap's day. To be sure, many of the accoutrements of the valley—bridges, highways, buildings, motorboats, restaurants—signify a modern world. The modern decorates but does not mask the true beauty—the overwhelming sense of human and natural history—that the Piscataqua and its tributaries impose upon the observer. The roar of motorboats, the huge cranes at the naval shipyard, the recurrent horn blowing when the Memorial Bridge rises and falls for passing tall ships, the crowded fishing boats preparing to depart and the endless traffic of tourists cannot interrupt the sublime experience of the foggy morning on Portsmouth harbor, the gentle sound of the river currents hidden by the gray mist. The competing smells of harbor restaurants, diesel from boats and the rank marsh are forgotten when the cool, saline zephyr ascends the Piscataqua. The vastness of the distant Atlantic seen from the open mouth of the Piscataqua makes the grandest tanker seem but a toy on an immense pond. The churning currents of the river continue to defy the ablest mariner with GPS, radar and diesel motor. The purplish water of the harbor as the sun declines in the evening, the blue of the tributaries on sunny days, the deep verdure of the forest enclosing the Oyster, Cocheco, Lamprey and other tributaries on rainy days, are the true colors of the Piscataqua, rather than the dull, rusted tankers, the old water tanks, the gaudy-colored fishing boats, the iron bridges, the rotting wharves. Interspersed among the heavy traffic, housing developments, tourist traps and shopping malls is the forest. The forest is inexorably a part of the Piscataqua. The white pine, pitch pine, hemlock, birch bark, ash and oak form the canopy on narrow byways, crowd about the shores of silent ponds, stand imposing along interstate highways, and make even swampy waste land majestic, serene and eerie.

A voyage up the Piscataqua is a voyage into the natural and human past. The rocky shore and headlands jutting into the sea greet today's mariner. Whaleback Light, which dates to the early 1800s, warns the mariner away from shoals at the mouth of the Piscataqua. Entering the broad mouth between Odiorne Point and Gerrish Island, the mariner sails into the narrow channel guarded by two forts. Fort Point, the site of Fort William and Mary and Fort Constitution, juts into the Piscataqua; the peninsula is warned by the lighthouse, originally established in 1771, which is in its third century of warning mariners away from the rocky point that now serves as a coast guard station. On the Maine side of the channel are the remains of Fort McClary on Kittery Point, which during its heyday in the mid-nineteenth century was a formidable bastion of defense for the Piscataqua Valley. With Newcastle, the Great Island, to the south and Seavey's Island, where the Portsmouth Naval Shipyard is located, to the north, the mariner ascends the narrow channel past the site of Fort Washington on Peirce's Island, arriving at Strawbery Banke. Prescott Park and Strawbery Banke Museum occupy the site where once was the liveliest port north of Boston. Tall ships sailed into harbor and unloaded cargo at Puddle Dock, a small inlet surrounded by merchants' homes and wharves. Looking out upon the water is the oldest graveyard in Portsmouth, called the Point of Graves, which dates back to the 1600s. Its age is such that over a century ago, when Thomas Aldrich roamed the yard, he was impressed by its antiquity.

Point of Graves, Strawbery Banke. Captain John Pickering donated land for the first graveyard in Portsmouth, as seen in this print from the early 1900s. *From* Vignettes of Portsmouth.

This military prison, on an island in the Piscataqua, is now abandoned, but from 1908 to 1974 held court-martialed navy prisoners. *Courtesy of Benjamin Lawson.*

It is an odd-shaped lot [he wrote], *comprising about half an acre, inclosed by a crumbling red brick wall two or three feet high, with wood capping. The place is overgrown with thistles, rank grass, and fungi; the black slate headstones have mostly fallen over; those that still make a pretense of standing slant to every point of the compass, and look as if they were being blown this way and that by a mysterious gale which leaves everything else untouched; the mounds have sunk to the common level, and the old underground tombs have collapsed. Here and there among the moss and weeds you can pick out some name that shines in the history of the early settlement; hundreds of the flower of the colony lie here, but the known and the unknown, gentle and simple, mingle their dust on a perfect equality now. The marble that once bore a haughty coat of arms is as smooth as the humblest slate stone guiltless of heraldry. The lion and the unicorn, wherever they appear on some cracked slab, are very much tamed by time. The once fat-faced cherubs, with wing at either cheek, are the merest skeletons now. Pride, pomp, grief, and remembrance are all at end. No reverent feet come here, no tears fall here; the old graveyard itself is dead! A more dismal, uncanny spot than this at twilight would be hard to find.*

Across the river one spies Kittery, the Portsmouth Naval Shipyard and Badger's Island, once a place where shipbuilders such William and Samuel Badger worked their art. Today's mariner sailing a mast ship ascends the Piscataqua under Memorial Bridge, a truss lift bridge that punctually rises every half hour. The remains of the first bridges to span the Piscataqua at this point have long disappeared, replaced in 1923 by this steel bridge, which memorializes those who fought in World War I, and which serves as the main local route for pedestrians and automobiles to come and go between Portsmouth and Kittery. Fishmongers calling out the daily price of fish have been replaced by restaurants at the water's edge where the dining experience is enlivened by the activity of the river: tugboats departing to escort a tanker lying in wait at the mouth of the Piscataqua; fishing and lobster boats returning with the day's catch; pleasure boats cruising back and forth; the harbor patrol keeping the peace; tour boats loaded with visitors, their cameras busy, the smell of diesel ubiquitous.

From Strawbery Banke the mariner proceeds up the Piscataqua, negotiating the Narrows, where the current is lively, between the towns of Newington on the New Hampshire side and Eliot on the Maine side. Eventually the river widens and a head of land divides the current. Here, at Dover Point, Edward Hilton established a fishing operation, bringing the catch of the day to port, splitting open the fish and setting them on flakes to dry in the sun and wind, which at the point is rarely still. A park named for Hilton occupies the site today. The point divides the Piscataqua, descending from the north, and the waters of the Little Bay and Great Bay, arriving from the west. Two bridges, one for autos and one for pedestrians, span the confluence of these various waters, where the current is rapid and swirling. The bridges stand where two hundred years ago the Piscataqua Bridge linked Bloody Point (Newington) with Dover Point. Previous to the Piscataqua Bridge, built in 1794, the traveler's only recourse to crossing the waters was Knight's Ferry, which operated during the Revolutionary years, and before that, anonymous entrepreneurs willing to risk life and fortune ferrying travelers across the turbulent waters of the Piscataqua.

Conclusion

Fort Constitution was used for the last time to defend the Piscataqua Valley during World War II. *Courtesy of Benjamin Lawson.*

Mariners take either of two routes, westward leading to Little Bay, which opens to Great Bay, fed by the waters of the Bellamy, Oyster, Lamprey and Squamscot Rivers, or north following the Piscataqua to its confluence with the Cocheco, and farther north, Salmon Falls River. The Great Bay was once a center of shipbuilding activity, builders constructing the boat with the wood of the surrounding forest, then launching it. The boats would lie moored while there at anchor, or downstream at Portsmouth, the addition of rigging, masts, sails and, if necessary, guns would make the ship ready for sea. The concern today is not shipbuilding; rather, it is preserving the natural beauty of the Great Bay estuary, where numerous fowl live and breed. Up the Squamscot lies the modest town of Exeter, once a Revolutionary capital and shipbuilding center, then a minor factory town at the falls of the Squamscot and today a tourist town that hosts upscale cultural events and features Phillips Exeter Academy. Up the Lamprey lies Newmarket, its great factories of the 1800s now silenced, yet still imposing. Up the Oyster River stands Durham, the violent attacks of raiders during the European wars for empire forgotten and replaced with the peaceful pursuit of knowledge at the University of New Hampshire. Up the Bellamy, washing the western side of Dover Point, lie Madbury and Barrington. Should the mariner leave Dover Point traveling north, the blue waters of the Piscataqua will lead to the Cocheco, up which is the town of Dover. Today, Dover is a busy town focused on service industries, though the old factory structures, now converted to other uses, still dominate the town center. Farther up the Cocheco, the traveler arrives at Rochester, an old industrial town that lies at the foothills of the distant White Mountains.

Fishing and lobstering is still important to the Piscataqua economy, and boats of all sizes and colors fill the harbor. *Courtesy of Benjamin Lawson.*

Conclusion

Up the Piscataqua River, the mariner arrives at the confluence with the Salmon Falls (Newichawannock) River, the channel of which separates the towns of Rollingsford and Somersworth on the New Hampshire side and the Berwicks on the Maine side. Berwick Academy is beginning its third century (founded in 1791), educating youth to follow in the footsteps of such alumni as Sarah Orne Jewett. At the falls, salmon, once ubiquitous and satisfying the hunger of native tribes, have disappeared, a casualty of industrialization, development and population growth. Yet in the quiet of the night one might still hear the sounds of the past, such as "the river falls," which over a century ago in Sarah Orne Jewett's time, though less often today, are "almost always to be heard by day, when one stops to listen, and loudest and most jarring in the dead of night to the wooden houses that vibrate to their constant notes."

Along the fall line of New Hampshire and Maine, the tributaries of the Piscataqua reach higher ground and powerful white water bars the path of mariners. Over the centuries the falls of the Squamscot, Lamprey, Cocheco and Newichawannock have provided Piscataqua inhabitants with the means of a secure livelihood, whether it be the plentiful fish that Indians and colonists caught or the power of the falls to turn waterwheels to power grist and lumber mills and turbines to generate hydroelectricity. The people and technology have changed over time. Unchanging is the river that gathers the waters of highlands and brings them together into one source, with each mile growing larger, stronger, until it reaches its destination and becomes one with the sea.

BIBLIOGRAPHY

PUBLISHED AND UNPUBLISHED DOCUMENTS

Batchellor, Albert S., et al., eds. *Laws of New Hampshire, Provincial Period*. 3 vols. Manchester, NH: 1904–1915.

Baxter, James P., ed. *Documentary History of the State of Maine*. 16 vols. Portland, ME: Lefavor-Tower, 1907–1916.

Belknap Papers. *Collections of the Massachusetts Historical Society*. Series 5, volumes 2 and 3. Series 6, volume 4. Boston: Massachusetts Historical Society, 1877, 1882, 1891.

Bouton, Nathaniel, et al. *Documents and Records Relating to the Province of New-Hampshire*. 40 vols. Concord, NH: Jenks, 1867–1943.

Collections of the Dover, New Hampshire, Historical Society. Volume 1. Dover, NH: Sales & Quimby, 1894.

Portsmouth Town Records. Typescript. Portsmouth, NH: Portsmouth Public Library.

PERIODICALS

Alden, Timothy. "Account of Religious Societies in Portsmouth." *Collections of the Massachusetts Historical Society*. Ser. 1. Vol. 10.

Dodge, Levi W. "Colonel Joseph Whipple and his Dartmouth Plantation." *Granite Monthly*, January 1893.

Jewett, Sarah Orne. "The Old Town of Berwick." *New England Magazine* 16 (1894). Now available online, http://www.public.coe.edu/~theller/soj/una/berwick.htm.

Lawson, Russell. "Essays on Man: The Belknap-Hazard Correspondence." *Historical New Hampshire* 52 (1997).

New Hampshire Gazette, 1756–1789.

"Sir William Pepperrell." *Sprague's Journal of Maine History* 7 (1919).

BOOKS

Adams, John P. *Drowned Valley*. Hanover, NH: University Press of New England, 1976.

Adams, Nathaniel. *Annals of Portsmouth*. Portsmouth, NH: Nathaniel Adams, 1825.

Aldrich, Thomas B. *An Old Town by the Sea*. New York: Houghton Mifflin, 1893.

Belknap, Jeremy. *The History of New-Hampshire*. 3 vols. Philadelphia and Boston: Aitken, Thomas and Andrew, 1784, 1791, 1792.

Benton, Josiah H. *Warning Out in New England*. Boston: Clarke, 1911.

Brewster, Charles W. *Rambles about Portsmouth*. Portsmouth, NH: Charles W. Brewster, 1859.

Burroughs, Charles. *Discourse Delivered in the Chapel of the New Almshouse, in Portsmouth, New Hampshire*. Portsmouth, NH: Foster, 1835.

Champlain, Samuel de. *Voyages*. Kessinger Publishing, 2004.

Clark, Charles. *The Eastern Frontier: The Settlement of Northern New England, 1610–1763*. Hanover, NH: University Press of New England, 1983.

———. *Maine: A History*. New York: W.W. Norton, 1977.

Clark, Frank E. and MaryBeth Faucher. *Around Somersworth*. Dover, NH: Arcadia, 1995.

Daniell, Jere R. *Colonial New Hampshire: A History*. Millwood, NY: KTO Press, 1981.

———. *Experiment in Republicanism: New Hampshire Politics and the American Revolution, 1741–1794*. Cambridge: Harvard University Press, 1970.

Dictionary of United States History: The New England States. 2 vols. Murietta, CA: U.S. History Publishers, 2006.

Dolph, James and Ronan Donohoe. *Around Portsmouth in the Victorian Era*. Dover, NH: Arcadia, 1997.

Duncan, Roger F. *Coastal Maine: A Maritime History*. Woodstock, VT. Countryman Press, 1992.

Encyclopedia of New England. Edited by Burt Feintuch and David H. Watters. New Haven: Yale University Press, 2005.

Fairchild, Byron. *Messrs. William Pepperrell: Merchants of Piscataqua*. Ithaca, NY: Cornell University Press, 1954.

Garvin, Donna-Belle, and James L. Garvin. *On the Road North of Boston: New Hampshire Taverns and Turnpikes, 1700–1900*. Concord: New Hampshire Historical Society, 1988.

Gyles, John. *Memoirs of Odd Adventures, Strange Deliverances, &c. In the Captivity of John Gyles, Esq.* Boston: Kneeland and Green, 1736.

Hosmer, James K., ed. *Winthrop's Journal: "History of New England," 1630–1649*. 2 vols. New York: Charles Scribner's Sons, 1908.

Hubbard, William. *General History of New England*. In *Collections of the Massachusetts Historical Society*. Series 2, Volumes 5 and 6. Boston: Massachusetts Historical Society, 1815. Reprint, New York: Johnson Reprint Corp., 1968.

Jordan, Chester B. *Colonel Joseph B. Whipple*. Concord, NH: Republican Press Association, 1894.

Josselyn, John. *New-Englands Rarities Discovered*. London: G. Widdowes, 1672.

Judd, R.W., E.A. Churchill and J.W. Eastman. *Maine: The Pine Tree State*. Orono, ME: University of Maine Press, 1995.

Kilbourne, Frederick W. *Chronicles of the White Mountains*. New York: Houghton Mifflin, 1916.

Kirsch, George B. *Jeremy Belknap: A Biography*. New York: Arno Press, 1982.

Knoblock, Glenn A. *Historic Burial Grounds of the New Hampshire Seacoast*. Charleston, SC: Arcadia, 1999.

Lawson, Russell M. *The American Plutarch: Jeremy Belknap and the Historian's Dialogue with the Past*. Westport, CT: Praeger, 1998.

———. *On the Road Histories: New Hampshire*. Northampton, MA: Interlink, 2006.

———. *Passaconaway's Realm: Captain John Evans and the Exploration of Mount Washington*. Hanover, NH: University Press of New England, 2002.

———. *Portsmouth: An Old Town by the Sea*. Charleston, SC: Arcadia, 2003.

Lindholdt, Paul, ed. *John Josselyn, Colonial Traveler: A Critical Edition of Two Voyages to New-England*. Hanover, NH: University Press of New England, 1988.

Marcou, Jane Belknap. *Life of Jeremy Belknap, D.D.: The Historian of New Hampshire*. New York: Harper Brothers, 1847.

Mayo, Lawrence Shaw. *John Langdon of New Hampshire*. Port Washington, NY: Kennikat Press, 1970.

McDuffee, Franklin. *History of Rochester*. Vol. 1. Manchester, NH: J.B. Clarke, 1892.

Morison, Samuel E. *John Paul Jones: A Sailor's Biography*. Boston: Little, Brown, 1959.

Page, Elwin L. *George Washington in New Hampshire*. Boston: Houghton Mifflin, 1932.

Pearson, Helen, and Harold H. Bennett. *Vignettes of Portsmouth*. Portsmouth, NH: Helen Pearson and Harold H. Bennett, 1913.

Penhallow, Samuel. *The History of the Wars of New-England with the Eastern Indians*. Boston: Fleet, 1726.

Potter, C.E. *The History of Manchester*. Manchester, NH: C.E. Potter, 1856.

Preble, Henry, and Walter C. Green. *Diary of Ezra Green, M.D.* Boston: Clapp, 1875.

Preston, Richard A. *Gorges of Plymouth Fort*. Toronto: University of Toronto Press, 1953.

Quint, Alonzo H. *The First Parish in Dover, New Hampshire*. Dover, NH: Mudge, 1884.

Rogers, Robert. *A Concise Account of North America*. London: J. Millan, 1765.

Ross, William E., and Thomas M. House. *Durham: A Century in Photographs*. Dover, NH: Arcadia, 1996.

Russell, Howard. *Indian New England before the Mayflower*. Hanover: University Press of New England, 1980.

Saltonstall, William G. *Ports of Piscataqua*. New York: Russell, 1968.

Smith, John. *The Complete Works of Captain John Smith*. Edited by Philip Barbour. 3 vols. Chapel Hill: University of North Carolina Press, 1986.

Stevens, Samuel C. *Sketch of Dover, N.H.: Topographical, Historical, Ecclesiastical, Statistical, & c. From the earliest period to the present time*. Dover, NH: Samuel C. Stevens, 1833.

Sullivan, James. *History of the District of Maine*. Boston: Thomas and Andrews, 1795.

Sullivan, John. *Letters and Papers of Major-General John Sullivan, Continental Army*. 3 vols. Concord, NH: New Hampshire Historical Society, 1930–1939.

Thomas, Matthew. *Rockingham County*. Augusta, ME: Alan Sutton, 1994.

Thompson, Mary P. *Landmarks in Ancient Dover, New Hampshire*. Durham, NH: Durham Historic Association, 1965.

Van Deventer, David. *The Emergence of Provincial New Hampshire, 1623–1741*. Baltimore: Johns Hopkins, 1976.

Varney, George J. *A Gazetteer of the State of Maine*. Boston: Russell, 1886.

Varrell, William. *Rye and Rye Beach*. Dover, NH: Arcadia, 1995.

"The Voyage of Martin Pring." *American Journeys Collection*. Madison: Wisconsin Historical Society, 2003.

Warren, William T., and Constance S. Warren. *Then & Now: Portsmouth*. Charleston, SC: Arcadia, 2001.

Whipple, Joseph. *The History of Acadie, Penobscot Bay and River*. Bangor, ME: Peter Edes, 1816.

Whittaker, Robert H. *Land of Lost Content: The Piscataqua River Basin and the Isles of Shoals. The People. Their Dreams. Their History*. Dover, NH: Alan Sutton, 1993.

Williamson, William D. *The History of the State of Maine*. Hallowell, ME: Glazier, Masters, 1832.

WEBSITES

American Lighthouse Foundation. http://www.lighthousefoundation.org.

Gulf of Maine Research Institute. http://www.gma.org.

Maine Historical Society. http://www.mainehistory.org.

Maine Memory Network. http://www.mainememory.net.

Portsmouth Gundalow Company. http://www.gundalow.org.

Portsmouth Naval Shipyard. http://www.ports.navy.mil.

SeacoastNH.com. http://www.seacoastnh.com.

Strawbery Banke Museum. http://www.strawberybanke.org.

Visit us at
www.historypress.net